The bombing of Dolphin's Ba   Dublin, 1941

WITHDRAWN

Maynooth Studies in Local History

SERIES EDITOR Raymond Gillespie

This volume is one of six short books published in the Maynooth Studies in Local History series in 2010. Like over 85 of their predecessors they range widely over the local experience in the Irish past. That local experience is presented in the complex social world of which it is part, from the world of the dispossessed Irish in 17th-century Donegal to political events in 1830s Carlow; from the luxury of the early 19th-century Dublin middle class to the poverty of the Famine in Tipperary; and from the political activists in Kimmage in 1916 to those who suffered in a different sort of war as their homes were bombed in South Circular Road in 1941. These local experiences cannot be a simple chronicling of events relating to an area within administrative or geographically determined boundaries since understanding the local world presents much more complex challenges for the historian. It is a reconstruction of the socially diverse worlds of poor and rich as well as those who took very different positions on the political issues that preoccupied the local societies of Ireland. Reconstructing such diverse local worlds relies on understanding of what the people of the different communities that made up the localities of Ireland had in common and what drove them apart. Understanding the assumptions, often unspoken, around which these local societies operated is the key to recreating the world of the Irish past and reconstructing the way in which those who inhabited those worlds lived their daily lives. As such, studies such as those presented in these short books, together with their predecessors, are at the forefront of Irish historical research and represent some of the most innovative and exciting work being undertaken in Irish history today. They also provide models which others can follow up and adapt in their own studies of the Irish past. In such ways will we understand better the regional diversity of Ireland and the social and cultural basis for that diversity. If they also convey something of the vibrancy and excitement of the world of Irish local history today they will have achieved at least some of their purpose.

Maynooth Studies in Local History: Number 90

The bombing of Dolphin's Barn, Dublin, 1941

Eoin C. Bairéad

FOUR COURTS PRESS

Set in 10pt on 12pt Bembo by
Carrigboy Typesetting Services for
FOUR COURTS PRESS LTD
7 Malpas Street, Dublin 8, Ireland
www.fourcourtspress.ie
and in North America for
FOUR COURTS PRESS
c/o ISBS, 920 N.E. 58th Avenue, Suite 300, Portland, OR 97213.

ISBN 978–1–84682–261–2

Printed in Scotland
by Thomson Litho, Glasgow.

Contents

Acknowledgments

Firstly I would like to thank Professor Raymond Gillespie for suggesting the idea for this study. Our first house as a family was in the Tenters' Fields, minutes from Donore Terrace, and that gave the project an immediacy it might otherwise have lacked. I must also thank Dr Ian Speller, whose insights and suggestions were given with kindness and humour and without whose help this work would have been considerably less coherent. Thanks are also due to Dr Mary Clark, the Dublin City Archivist and Dr Máire Kennedy, the Divisional Librarian for Special Collections in Dublin City Libraries; to all the staff in Dublin City Library and Archive, Pearse Street; to the National Archives of Ireland and the Director of the National Archives of Ireland; and to the Officer-in-Charge and the staff in the Irish Military Archives, Cathal Brugha Barracks, Rathmines, Dublin 6.

A special thanks must go to four people who received me into their homes with welcome and kindness and who shared with me their memories of a Dublin of 70 years before: Jack Earley, Paddy Culligan and Finlay and Chris Myles. The primary source for this work is the bureaucratic record of a civic authority. These four reminded me that it was above all a human story.

Finally, thanks are due to Professor Gillespie, Dr Terence Dooley and Mr Rob Goodbody of the Department of History, NUI Maynooth, for two years of informative, educational, stimulating and above all entertaining studies. Go raibh míle maith agaibh go léir.

'WW2 People's War' is an online archive of wartime memories contributed by members of the public and gathered by the BBC. The archive can be found at bbc.co.uk/ww2peopleswar/

Newspaper photographs of the period are published with the kind permission of Irish Press Ltd.

The photograph of the bomb fragment was obtained from and is printed with the kind permission of the Irish Military Archives, Cathal Brugha Barracks, Dublin.

Figure 1 is reproduced by permission of Ordnance Survey Ireland, Copyright Permit No. MP 000810.

Introduction

On the first three days of January 1941, German bombs were dropped at a number of locations along the east coast of Ireland, including counties Carlow, Kildare, Louth, Meath, Wexford and Wicklow. On successive nights, 2 and 3 January 1941, Dublin City was attacked for the first time, with incidents in Terenure and then on the South Circular Road, where a twin row of houses named Donore Terrace was struck. This work will examine the response of Dublin Corporation to the latter bombing, concentrating particularly on the efforts of the Corporation to limit and control the costs incurred in responding to the affair, and the parallel efforts of those affected to ensure that they were adequately compensated for all damage done to their property.

Beginning on the very morning of the bombing itself the Corporation activated a plan for structural repairs to damaged property; later it administered the Irish government's scheme of compensation under the Neutrality (War Damage to Property) Act, 1941. The relevant files were transferred to the Dublin City Archives under the 60-year rule. They describe the process of repair, reconstruction and compensation as well as giving a vivid picture of the efforts of the householders to ensure that this was done to their complete satisfaction, irrespective of the views of Corporation officials.

Given that there were no deaths, and that the injuries, though serious, were not life-threatening, it could be felt that the incident does not merit any form of historical analysis. However, it is hoped that, by presenting an examination of both primary and secondary source material, a different conclusion might be reached.

According to a 'traditional' view, what happened in Dublin in 1941 was not 'history' in the true meaning of that word. With the confidence one expects of the Regius Professor of Modern History at Oxford, Edward Freeman could declare in 1884: 'History is past politics: politics is present history'.[1] While this view was challenged, particularly by French historians in the early 20th century, the proposition that history was somehow concerned with 'grand' events persisted, even in this 'new history'. Political decisions by important males were replaced as the subject matter of history by analysis of long-term socio-economic trends – the so-called *longue durée* approach.

A significant reaction to this *longue durée* view of history was what became known as microhistory. The German-US historian Georg G. Iggers in his work *Historiography in the twentieth century* stated that microhistory arose because the generalizations made, even in 'new history', did not stand up to rigorous analysis when measured against real individuals and the lives they actually lived.[2] Arising from this perceived failure, articles began to appear in journals focusing specifically on microhistorical research; the work of the Italian historian Carlo Ginzburg was central, primarily in the Italian journal *Quaderni Storici*, but also in the German journal *Historische Anthropologie*, and in English in the Chicago published *Critical Inquiry*.[3] Rather than the big economic picture microhistorians stress smaller units, often single individuals. This reduction of scale, microhistorians argue, permits them to dissect the individual relationships in all their complexity and through this analysis, to get a better, truer picture of the society in which those individuals lived, and, in a reflection of that image, to learn more about our own world today, and the role we play in it. They tend to focus on the less 'usual' individuals rather than the 'average', using the term 'normal exception' to describe those of whom they write.[4] As such, we can read of a murdered Gaelic historian, a heretical Italian miller, a French schoolmaster's dead cat, or a Tipperary woman who was burned to death because she had been 'exchanged for a fairy', all having been analysed using this methodology.[5]

It will be important, therefore, to show how the study of the individuals affected by the Donore bombings can provide more than a merely voyeuristic opportunity to examine the minutiae of those lives, and additionally to show how their responses to the disaster/inconvenience that was the bombing of January 1941 can resonate in the Dublin of nearly 70 years later. As stated, the main primary source is the Dublin City Council file of correspondence with affected residents, as well as internal notes and memoranda detailing the Corporation's response. These documents, coming as they do from the City Manager's department, are filed as *Donore area bombing 1941* – CMD/1941/1, and consist of five folders, referred to as File 1 to File 5. So as to avoid confusion between the file itself – CMD/1941/1 – and the individual sections, the term folder will be used throughout this work.

The folders, therefore, are:

> Folder no. 1: entitled *Air raid precaution reports* this small folder contains reports from Horace O'Rourke, Dublin city architect, to P.J. Hernon, the city manager and town clerk outlining air raid precautions, reporting on progress in clearing bomb damage and advising on precautions to be taken in case of future bomb attack on the city.

> Folder no. 2: entitled *Structural repair/demolition*, a large folder containing reports submitted to Hernon by O'Rourke on measures taken to repair property damaged in the bombing as well as letters from individuals who had lost property thereby and who were seeking compensation.

Folder no. 3: entitled *Reports on damage to property*, this folder consists of reports from assessors and surveyors appointed by Dublin Corporation to examine bomb damage to residential property.

Folder no. 4: entitled *Claims for compensation* this is the other big folder, and the most problematic. It contains correspondence with claimants, individual and corporate, for compensation under the Neutrality (War Damage to Property) Act, 1941. In other words, damage other than structural. The filing here is made more difficult to follow, paradoxically because some effort has been made to group together in bundles all correspondence relating to a single property or concerning particular or similar individuals. There is, for instance, a small bundle dealing with damage to the National Boxing Stadium. The problem is, however, that it is difficult to organize the many bundles in a coherent fashion.

Folder no. 5: entitled *Assessors' fees*, containing correspondence between quantity surveyors and assessors engaged by Dublin Corporation to report on bomb damage in the area.

Within the folders, the individual items, many of which lack unique identifiers, are either loose (as is the case with Folder 1), or grouped using clipper paper fasteners in what were probably considered manageable bundles. Frequently the latest item is at the top, and the bundle must be read in reverse order. Quite often there are multiple copies of the same document, not always filed contiguously, and sometimes in different folders.

While it is self-evident that correspondence received from the affected Dubliners is clearly written with the explicit purpose of presenting their side of the story, it might be assumed that the information given by the Corporation was accurate, unbiased and authoritative. However, it is important to realize that as with all documents, official or otherwise, while these are quintessentially 'official' they were nonetheless compiled for and by individuals – people who, like anyone else doing a job, saw it as important that the data were presented in a way that both justified their own analysis of events and, equally importantly, showed that they were managing those events and their consequences in a professional and efficient fashion.

A perhaps more objective view of this story might be acquired from the second major primary source – the newspapers (national, other Irish and foreign) of the time. As with the Corporation files, it might be questioned whether these give an account of the events that is 'accurate, unbiased and authoritative'. What they do give is a picture of how the incident was reported by the press, and how it was presented to ordinary readers both in Ireland and abroad. This may not be how it was seen by either the authorities or the residents, but it is nonetheless valid to the area of study. It must be stated that, contrary to anecdotal records of the period, the coverage in the newspapers was extensive and detailed, and photographs were widely used to show the scenes of destruction. Identification of the bombs as being German was explicit, both in Irish[6] and English publications. There is no hint of extensive censorship.

The last main primary source relative to the bombing and the Corporation's response is the equivalent Dublin Corporation folders on events of the following May: the bombing of North Strand.[7] Study of these files will clarify whether the authorities reacted differently to this second, much greater, tragedy. In particular it will be seen if the Corporation's initial reaction had changed, if emergency services were deployed differently, if the immediate response to damage done to property differed materially in the two incidents, and, what might be most interesting of all, to see if the pledges of compensation and the method of assessing it were amended in the light of the experiences of the Donore bombing.

There are two other primary documentary sources that will be used. The Irish army played a central role in the military response to this and all other bombings in the state during the war. The files recording this response, grouped in a box called 'Second World War bombings', are held in the Military Archives in Cathal Brugha Barracks, Rathmines, Dublin. Finally the affected residents, particularly when they felt that extra assistance was called for, wrote to various government departments; this correspondence is in the National Archives in Bishop Street, Dublin.

Lastly, a valid, if problematical, primary source of these events is the reminiscences by people who actually experienced the bombing. The issue of 'oral history' is often difficult, with some historians categorizing it as folklore, and others emphasizing its central importance in coming to a true and full understanding of events in the past. Formally, oral history can be defined as the recording, preservation and interpretation of historical information, based on the personal experiences and opinions of an individual or individuals. Its proponents see it as a vital tool for our understanding of the recent past, and as complementing rather than replacing the established methodologies. On a more political level, it is often seen as enabling those who might not have featured in more traditional historiography to be recorded, as well as a means whereby those interested in the past can record their own personal experiences and those of their families and communities.

Standard textbooks on oral history paint an understandably positive picture of its use:

> The strength of oral history lies in the fact that it complements written, printed and visual sources and can often clearly call into question those

other sources. It can be, and often is, a fundamental method of acquiring information that cannot be obtained in any other way. For the heritage professional to ignore oral history would be like a general under enemy fire deciding not to use tanks because they are a little time-consuming and somewhat noisy. His lack of appropriate action will be judged by posterity.[8]

The special care and attention this type of history requires is, unhappily, exemplified by the same author, a few pages later, repeating the old canard that the children's rhyme 'Ring-a-ring-a-roses' has its origins in some long gone plague.[9] Whatever view one takes, personal reminiscences are not without historical value, and it is important to capture the memories of those who lived through the period and weave their story into the account.

In addition to these primary sources, there is much secondary literature on the period. A work submitted to NUI Maynooth in July 2002 by Jennifer Duffy as her M.A. thesis entitled 'The Corporation of Dublin and the bombing of the North Strand, 31 May 1941' is a most valuable source of material that allows a comparison to be made between that May event and the one – nearly five months earlier –under discussion in the present work.[10] While only two of the printed secondary sources mention the Donore bombing, this secondary literature does permit the building of a picture of the Dublin of the 1940s.[11] What even a cursory reading of this literature shows is that there were two Dublins, and that the interaction and mutual awareness between them was minimal. Tony Gray in his work on *The Emergency* paints a slightly rosy picture of those years in 'Eire' (consistently without the accent), as he calls it.[12] Gray quotes from Garret FitzGerald's autobiography *All in a life*, a passage well known enough to merit giving a small extract:

> An element of student life in that period was the formal dance, most commonly in the Gresham Hotel and organized by the past pupils of a secondary school or by a charity, which included dinner during the evening. White tie and tails were appropriate for these occasions, with black tie for the dinnerless five-shilling Saturday-night dances.

> A feature of these dances was that many of us travelled to and from them by bicycle, often with a girl on the crossbar, her ball-gown packed away in a carrier-basket; it was necessary for the girls to change at the dance if they were to have a safe bicycle journey home in a shorter skirt.[13]

Even outsiders thought life here at the time to be pleasant and enjoyable – Helen Litton quotes a Swiss newspaper:

To anyone privileged to leave the warlike atmosphere of England and visit Ireland ... it seems as if one has moved into an unreal world ... above all the peaceful routine and the enjoyment of leisurely gossip remind the visitor of long forgotten times.[14]

And yet it should be immediately clear that this picture is not just incomplete – it is seriously flawed. Can one imagine the residents of the new suburb of Crumlin, the then 20-years-old Corporation purchase schemes in the Tenters' Fields, and those living in artisans' cottages in Harolds' Cross or the Liberties – all of the above in the area affected by the bombs – cycling to dress dances with their 'white ties and tails' on a regular basis?

The status of the poor in Dublin, and indeed in the entire country, is described with almost clinical precision in James Meenan's essay on the Irish economy during the war, which appears in the Thomas Davis series on *Ireland in the war years*. Meenan describes how loss of markets, lower prices for exports, higher costs of imports, massive unemployment, and inadequate or non-existent investment in infrastructure all contributed to a period of intense hardship for a huge percentage of the people: 'the shortage of raw materials affected every part of national life' while 'the cost of living index ... had been 173 in 1938. By 1943 it had risen to 284 – and at that time it was only on the threshold of really sharp annual increases' and 'many factories had to close down altogether'.[15]

However, Donore Terrace was not poor, and its residents not destitute. It was a comfortably well-off middle-class community, confident of its place in society and confident in its own self-worth. That confidence would play a major role in how those Dubliners dealt with the bombing of their neighbourhood. The present work begins with a brief description of Donore Terrace and a profile of its residents. The next chapter describes the bombing itself and the period directly afterwards, detailing the immediate response of the Corporation as well as the initial reaction of the affected citizens. The third chapter considers the interaction between the Corporation and the residents, the efforts taken by the latter to achieve their aim of minimizing financial loss, and the attempts by the former to control, as far as possible, the costs involved. There follows a chapter on the folklore surrounding the event and interviews with four individuals who remembered it, as well as a brief mention of the Corporation's role during the bombing of Belfast in April 1941. The work concludes with a description of the aftermath of the bombing, considering both how the experience helped shape the response of the Corporation to the far more serious bombing in North Strand the following May, and the fall-out within that organization itself as a result of its handling of the Donore bombing.

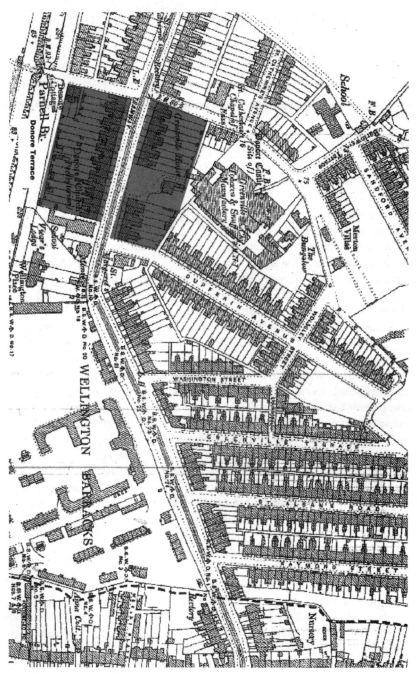

1 Map of Donore Terrace. © Ordnance Survey Ireland, permit no. MP 000810

1. Donore Terrace, a brief history

As one goes along the South Circular Road in Dublin westward from Clanbrassil Street and Leonard's Corner, one will notice, just past the National [Boxing] Stadium and the old Presbyterian Church (now a mosque), two terraces of Victorian red-bricked houses, left and right. Apart from two of their number, the houses on the left side all have bay windows. On the right is a large commercial building with plastered pock marks in the façade; if one looks more closely, one will notice that the ground floor windows of this building have stars of David as a motif.

In 1941 the houses on both sides were known as Donore Terrace[1], and in the early morning of 3 January 1941 a German plane dropped two high explosive bombs on the southern side of the road, damaging the entire terrace and demolishing two houses. Twenty-four-hours earlier bombs had been dropped in Terenure, a few kilometres to the south.

A pair of demolished houses on the left was rebuilt, but without bay windows; the building on the right was at the time the Greenville Hall Synagogue, hence the stars of David. The Irish Government was subsequently repaid by the German authorities for the damage caused on that night – a fact that has led the local people to say with some pride that theirs was the only synagogue in Europe bombed by the Nazis for which the Germans paid compensation! The terrace runs from the mosque to Donore Avenue; at the time of the bombing there were 35 houses on it, running from nos. 85 to 119, as well as the church and the synagogue, now headquarters of Mason Technology.

The first appearance of the terrace in *Thom's Dublin Directory* is in 1881, where four houses, three vacant, are shown 'between the Richmond Bridewell[2] and Sally's Bridge'.[3] This would imply that the houses were finished the previous year (1880). In the following edition of the directory, there are nine houses and the Presbyterian church; the next edition has eleven, and in 1884 there were 25 houses, all included in the general heading 'South Circular Road'. The south side of the terrace is shown as complete in the 1885 edition. Over the next decade or so, the north side was built; originally styled Chaworth Terrace, finally named Donore Terrace, and shown as complete in the 1897 edition of *Thom's*. It may be taken, therefore, that the terrace was built in two halves – the earlier, southern, part built quickly over four years, and the northern side in a more leisurely fashion over 14 years.

With the exception of two properties, the houses were valued (according to *Thom's*) at between £23 and £28; no. 119 was valued at £30, and no. 102

2 Donore Terrace today

stood out at £40. The latter, however, was Greenville House, appearing as a
separate property when building work began, and occupied by William Dunne,
who was also shown as the occupier (briefly) of no. 97 opposite. By way of
comparison, the valuations in nearby streets show the slightly superior nature
of the Donore houses. In Heytesbury Street, just across Clanbrassil Street to
the east, the average valuation was £19. In both Dufferin Avenue and Donore
Avenue, roads to the immediate east and west of Donore Terrace, the houses
were assessed at between £17 and £23.[4]

A second source of statistics is the 1911 census, taken on the night of 2
April of that year.[5] First, all of the houses on the terrace are shown as '2nd
class' on the 'House and Building return (Form B)'. This in no way implies
inferiority – the mark assigned to each house was 11, the maximum for this
class.[6] There were 179 people living in 39 dwellings on the terrace – no. 89
was shown as three units and no. 91 as two. Four of the houses were shown
as empty. The house with most inhabitants was no. 119 with 11 people; it will
be remembered that this was one of the pair of unusually high valuations. 16
of the households had six or more people in them. The average age of those
staying on the terrace was just over 30 – certainly not a community of young
families, but nonetheless, not elderly. Lucinda Reddy in no. 91 was the eldest
at 80, and seven were children under 5.

The religious make-up of the terrace was interesting as much for the
descriptions used by the individuals as the sectarian break-down itself. There

3 Greenville Hall Synagogue today

were 62 'Roman' Catholics and two 'Catholics'. There were 63 in communion with the See of Canterbury in some fashion or other, described variously as 'Church of Ireland' (45), 'Church of Ireland (Episcopalian)' (five), 'Church of England' (nine), 'Episcopalian' (one), and 'Irish Church' (three). There were also 22 Presbyterians, 11 Baptists and one Methodist. Given the reputation of the area as 'Dublin's Little Jerusalem', the fact that there were only 18 'Hebrews' in four families in three adjoining households (nos. 90, 92 and 94) may be remarked on.

The gender breakdown was 74 males and 105 females – a statistically significant difference. Some can be explained if we consider houses such as no. 92 with the Elyans, a Jewish family of five, and a single Roman Catholic female, Mary Casey, or their co-religionist neighbours in 94, the six Beckers and Rubenstiens, with, again, a single (16-year-old) Catholic female – Dolly Norah O'Brien. There was not a single exclusively male household in the 35 houses. There were, however, 13 houses with a female having a different surname (and often a different religion) to the rest of the household. Servants were not expensive in the Dublin of 1911. Seeing that there were some households *with* servants that were exclusively or almost exclusively female, it does appear that status rather than available hands was a defining factor. The four female Holdens in no. 114 (ranging in age from 23 to 56) still had Kate Corr working for them, and the five Misses Brown in 107, with ages from 27 to 36, had Annie Moran. Given that just over a third of the houses had such an extra female, we might make certain assumptions about the relative worth of the residents. For instance, against that 37 per cent with servants, there are two houses with definite multi-tenancies – 89 and 91 (because they were enumerated separately) – and a further six with more than two surnames. While this might represent an extended family, given that there were also religious differences it may be more realistic to consider that some houses were availing of extra income from lodgers (in spite of being classified on Form N (the enumerator's abstract) as being single 'families') and this number was about 60 per cent of those able to afford a servant.[7] While there were those on the terrace who found that extra source of income useful, the profile of the 35 houses would indicate that the residents were, in the main, comfortably well-off.

Dublin City Council has archived, and made available on-line, the voters' registers of the period, and these constitute another valuable source of information. While *Thom's* gives primarily occupiers of the terrace, these books give the owners, and, additionally, often give other premises owned by the same individuals, since at the time voting in municipal elections was the prerogative of rate payers.

One of the more valuable documents in the city manager's file is a list of all those residing on the terrace at the time of the bombing. It was compiled by A. Grimston, the area warden of the Air Raid Precaution Service (the ARP) for the area (area 10); although undated, it was probably made between 1 and 3 February 1941 as the documents on either side of the list in Folder 2 have those dates.[8] Stating where the residents had found alternative accommodation, this list shows both families that are large by today's standards and, again, houses which have lodgers or servants or both.[9] The names from these three sources – *Thom's* Directory, the Voters' register, and area warden Grimston's list – have been combined in Appendix 1.

There are two cases where we have fairly exact information on the income of residents. The house of George Day, no. 91, was one of the two destroyed in the bombing. The Days acquired alternative accommodation and petitioned for assistance in furnishing it. A condition of meeting this request was that a statement of income be provided. In a letter to him from the *Leas Rúnaidhe* (Assistant Secretary) of the Valuation Office, dated 17 April 1941, George Day was confirmed to be a Clerical Officer on an annual salary of £320 5s. 0d.[10] Another victim, Nellie Griffin, the maid in no. 89, subsequently sought recompense for loss of earnings consequential on being injured; her father's letter dated 12 March 1941 on her behalf says her pay was £1 10s. per month, or £18 per annum.[11] George Day made more in three weeks than Nellie Griffin did in a year – a ratio that shows the comfortable standing of the principal residents of Donore Terrace.

The statistics of the terrace show a respectable middle-class community living in houses that were similar in status and value, with a household size that shows a spread that might well be surprising today, but one that, 70 years ago, was not unusual. And, again not unusually for the period, some had lodgers, some had servants, and some, indeed, had both.

2. The bombing

The Second World War began on 3 September 1939 when the United Kingdom and France declared that they were at war with Germany. Most of the British Commonwealth issued similar declarations in the subsequent days and weeks. Uniquely within Commonwealth members, but along with most of Europe, Ireland declared itself neutral in the conflict.[1] However, its closeness to Britain, both geographically and demographically, made certain relationships and certain incidents almost inevitable. Indeed, Garret FitzGerald's suggestion that Ireland should be described as 'non-belligerent' rather than 'neutral' has much to recommend it.[2] In Ireland, the period of the war itself was referred to as 'The Emergency', since a state of such emergency was deemed legally necessary for the Oireachtas to be allowed pass certain legislation. The Taoiseach, Éamon de Valera, officially declared such to be the case in Dáil Éireann on 2 September 1939, moving 'that Dáil Éireann hereby resolves, pursuant to sub-section 3° of section 3 of Article 28 of the Constitution, that, arising out of the armed conflict now taking place in Europe, a national emergency exists affecting the vital interests of the State'. He went on to say 'I do not think it is necessary for me to add anything to what I have already said. I think it is evident to everybody that the circumstances contemplated by the amendment of the Article of the Constitution do, in fact, exist'.[3]

As Eunan O'Halpin describes the situation in *Defending Ireland*, the government basically accepted the conventional wisdom of the time that aerial bombing of civilian targets would be an inevitable and rapidly decisive tactic in the future European war.[4] This belief was both engendered and reinforced by the Luftwaffe's spectacular assaults against undefended towns during the Spanish civil war. And de Valera would have had access to first-hand information on these raids from two quite different sources – the volunteers for Eoin O'Duffy's Irish Brigade who fought with Franco, and their fellow countrymen, many old comrades of the Taoiseach's, who served with the International Brigade in the same conflict. In spite of its supposed antipathy to Britain, de Valera's government looked eastward for supplies, advice and example on how to prepare for war. An Air Raid Precautions Act was passed by the Oireachtas in July 1939, echoing much of the framework laid down in the UK legislation of 18 months previously, their Air Raid Precautions Act 1937.[5] The Irish Government's one penny booklet, entitled *The protection of your home against air raids*, explicitly acknowledges the indebtedness of the Aire

Cosanta (Minister for Defence) to the Controller of the British Stationery Office for 'basing' the Irish book on the British Home Office publication of exactly the same name.[6]

The Irish act also provided for a civil defence framework based on local authorities, and volunteer corps known as the ARP (Air Raid Precautions) were set up by these county councils and corporations, beginning almost immediately. Larger authorities, such as Dublin Corporation, had full-time officials running the ARP, and training began there in September 1939.[7] Unfortunately, almost no records seem to have been kept in the city archives, although many hundreds of individuals, male and female, were members. The force was disbanded after the war, although the need for such an organization was acknowledged almost immediately, and Civil Defence was set up in 1950 under the same legislation.[8]

Apart from setting up the ARP, almost nothing was done before war was declared to prepare the public for possible aerial attack, to strengthen the fire and ambulance services or to train their personnel, to formulate plans for the evacuation and accommodation of civilians dislocated by bombing, or to secure communications systems from bomb damage. However, O'Halpin's analysis that 'all of this was left on one of the state's many long fingers until events overtook complacency' may be a little over-harsh, for, as will be seen, there were clearly individuals in Dublin Corporation who were aware of the dangers and conscious that a proper infrastructure, a well-thought-out plan and a clear sense of purpose were essential.[9] The lack of planning was not unique to the South; indeed, the state of preparedness in Belfast was described by one commentator as 'complacency and incompetence', and Jonathan Bardon's criticism is particularly excoriating.[10] While the minutiae of the Corporation response may well have left much to be desired, fortunately for Dublin the learning process was not dependent on events such as the Belfast Blitz of 15 and 16 April 1941.

This learning process began nearly a year after the war began. On Tuesday, 26 August 1940 in Co. Wexford, the railway viaduct at Ambrosetown and the home of James Hawkins and his wife in Duncormick, about five miles from Campile Creamery, were bombed.[11] Some damage was caused to the roof of the house but no one was injured. Shortly after, a device was dropped on the creamery itself at Campile and three women were killed. Uniquely in wartime bombings in the State, the Irish army was of the opinion that this bombing was deliberate. The report to the Chief of Staff by Commandant D.J. Murphy and Captain T.J. Hanley mentioned an earlier bombing of the Rosslare-Fishguard boat, and saw in the set of attacks an attempt by Germany to disrupt or destroy the supply of food to Britain, as well as a punishment for the breaking-off of trade with Germany by the creamery management in Campile.[12]

The Air Raid Precautions Act stated that 'the Minister with the concurrence of the Minister for Finance may, out of moneys provided by the

Oireachtas, provide such services, train such persons, and acquire such air raid precautions equipment, as he considers necessary for the purposes of affording protection to persons and property in the event of attack from the air, and lend, supply free of charge, or sell any such equipment'.[13] The Dublin Corporation official given overall responsibility for these precautions was the city architect, Horace Tennyson O'Rourke, a hugely important figure. His career as a corporation architect was a long one, starting in 1916 – it was he who designed O'Connell Street as it exists today, he who supervised its reconstruction after the destruction by the gunboat *Helga* in the 1916 Easter Rising, and he who was closely involved with Abercrombie, Kelly & Robertson's plan for the re-development of Dublin.[14] His superior, the city manager, was the equally significant Patrick J. Hernon. When Dublin Corporation was suspended (as a result of Civil War disagreements) from 1924 to 1930, it was replaced by three commissioners, one of whom was Hernon.[15] He was made city manager and town clerk, controversially and over the heads of the Corporation, in 1936.[16]

On 7 October 1940 O'Rourke wrote to Hernon.[17] In this memorandum he reported that the persons and equipment required by the Act were in place, but now, as city architect, he wished to consider the aftermath of an attack, and explicitly the need for repairs rather than demolition or rebuilding of affected buildings. Referring to the British model, the Housing (Emergency Powers) Act of 1939, he noted the obligation on local authorities there to repair such damaged buildings. Pointing out that a 'rescue and demolition service' was already in place in Dublin, he noted that its operations did not 'appear to extend to structural first-aid', and asked whether existing legislation could be extended to provide this service, or whether new legislation would be needed; it will be seen that the latter alternative was the one chosen.

O'Rourke then, with typical efficiency, detailed areas where these additional services should be organized, areas that could be resolved into three parts: (a) investigation and supervision, (b) labour and (c) materials. Under (a) a Supervising Officer would be allocated by the Corporation, and provided with the necessary technical assistance. Under (b) the local authority would consult in advance with master builders, trade unions and local employment exchanges, and he noted that, while the Corporation and these groups might already be familiar with rescue and demolition, repair would be much more complicated, involving 'almost entirely skilled labour'. Under (c) he proposed that the local authority would consult with the Government to draw on its own reserves, as private stocks would be 'uncertain'. He concluded 'the essential character of this additional service should be speed in organization, and this cannot be achieved without careful preliminary organization'. O'Rourke made it his job to see that this would be done.

O'Rourke's concerns became concrete three months later, with a fortnight of events beginning on Friday, 20 December 1940. That night two high

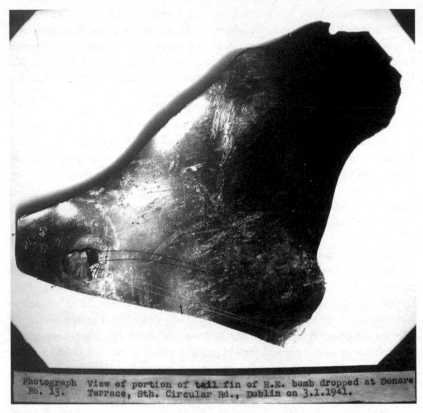

Photograph   View of portion of tail fin of H.E. bomb dropped at Donore
No. 13.   Terrace, Sth. Circular Rd., Dublin on 3.1.1941.

4 Bomb fragments

explosive bombs fell near Sandycove railway station and three people were injured.[18] Later the same evening Drumcera, near Carrickmacross, Co. Monaghan was the target.

Eleven days after the Sandymount and Monaghan bombings, in the first days of 1941, there was a far more concerted series of attacks.[19] On the morning of 1 January two magnetic mines were dropped near Kilmacanogue in Wicklow, but did not explode. That night, seven bombs were dropped near Drogheda, and two close to Bettystown. In the early hours of the next morning, 2 January, seven bombs fell on Terenure in Dublin, and three people were injured; eight bombs fell near the Curragh Racecourse, ten near Duleek and, in the worst incident, eight on Knockrow near Carlow where three people were killed. That evening three more bombs fell near Oylegate in Wexford.

Later that night, Dublin was bombed again:

At 03.55 hrs on the 3rd January (1941) two HE[20] bombs were dropped at Donore Terrace, SC Rd. Two houses in the Terrace (Nos. 91 and 93) were completely demolished and a number of houses and buildings in the vicinity were severely damaged. 22 persons were injured, none fatally. The bombs fell on either side of the two houses mentioned above. Fragments of HE bombs recovered from the scene bore markings indicative of German origin, for which see attached photographs numbered 12 and 14.

So reads the rather terse report in the Military Archives on the first major bombing in Dublin since the Rebellion of 1916.[21]

THE BOMBING ITSELF

'Nobody killed, many injured'. Thus read the sub-headline on page 5 of the *Irish Times* of 3 January 1941, appearing within hours of the actual event. It continued:

> ... a heavy calibre bomb demolished two houses and partly wrecked a third when it made a direct hit at Donore Terrace, South Circular Road, Dublin, at 3.56 o'clock this morning ... about 50 houses have suffered serious damage. Glass in hundreds of houses in the area has been blown out, and the blast was heard far beyond Harold's Cross Bridge.

The *Irish Independent* of the same day told how 'Guards, members of the LSF and ARP squads were quickly on the scene, and with the aid of residents, worked feverishly to free the trapped people'.[22] The *Independent* also gave extra details of those removed to the Meath Hospital. As well as the inhabitants of the two houses mentioned, M[olly] Miller of no. 92 and Mrs A. Green of no. 96, both on the terrace, were treated, as well as fireman Thomas Smart and Garda John Maguire, both injured in the rescue.[23]

The Commandant giving the military report provided further information.[24] Two houses, no. 91 (occupied by Mr Day and four others) and no. 93 (occupied by Mr Roith and eight others) were completely destroyed. Twenty-two persons were taken to hospitals, but he understood that the majority of them had already been discharged.

The ARP area warden, W.E. Hennessy, compiled a report on the same day which he sent to Colonel Thomas E. Gay (retired), the Air Raid Precautions Officer for the Corporation, in which he detailed the damage:

86 & 88	Windows broken, ceilings damaged, front door and stairs gone
90, 92, 94	Shambles
96	Badly damaged – part of roof gone
100	Synagogue – windows broken and door gone
102	Windows broken – ceilings damaged
104, 106, 108, 110, 112	Windows broken – ceilings damaged
114, 116, 118	Windows broken
83	Church attached (Presbyterian). Windows Broken, doors blown off. Ceilings badly damaged. School at rear – shambles
85 & 87	Ceilings damaged, walls damaged and windows broken
89	Semi-demolished (ruins)
91 & 93	Demolished
95	Semi-demolished (ruins)
97 & 99	Shambles
101 & 103	Windows broken, ceilings damaged, doors blown off
105, 107, 109, 111, 113, 115	Ceilings and walls damaged, windows broken

And he went on to say: 'windows broken and doors blown off in neighbouring streets'.[25]

By the following day, according to the *Irish Independent*, only seven people were still in hospital.[26] Less than a week later most were discharged, for on 9 January the Department of Defence sent a letter to the private secretary to the Taoiseach listing the casualties still in hospital as a result of 'the recent aerial bombing incidents'.[27] Four women from Donore Terrace were included – two of the Roith family (of 93), Mrs Day (of 91) and Mrs Ellison (of 88).

The job of rescue was facilitated by the fact that the local ARP post warden, Miss Maureen Whelan, had a notebook giving details of all those living in the houses, and this 'census' allowed rescuers to verify that all were accounted for.[28] While such manuscript notebooks were commonly kept by the ARP, what is possibly a unique surviving example is held in the Dublin City Archives.[29]

The *Irish Times* editorial of the following Saturday criticized the lack of warning given – that although unidentified aircraft were seen, no sirens were sounded.[30] The city manager's reply offers the best summary of the response to the bombing.

On the South Circular Road the air raid wardens were on the scene five minutes after the explosion occurred. Five minutes from then three of the injured had been rescued. In a further five minutes a total of eight of the injured had been rescued, and in very difficult circumstances the last two victims had been rescued inside half an hour from the time of the explosion … it is suggested to us that if the sirens were in operation valuable time could have been saved. No time was lost.[31]

It is difficult to find any newspaper reports of the bombing after that date, apart from photographs of the repairs and restoration.

A different angle, however, was taken in its edition of 5 January by the *Sunday Independent*.[32] Headed 'Can the bomb victims claim compensation?' an unnamed 'insurance representative' informed the unnamed reporter that no insurance company in Europe offered compensation for war damage of any kind. The reporter then went on to say that the question of war risk insurance had been raised in the Seanad some months previously, when it was promised on behalf of the Government that an announcement would be made 'in due course'.

This probably refers to one of two debates, both in Seanad Éireann, and both of which concerned insurance rather than compensation. In the adjournment debate on 29 May 1940, Mr Douglas raised the matter of War Risk Insurance in Éire, and in the debate on 25 September, 1940, in a formal motion on War Risk Insurance for Property, Mr M. Hayes moved 'That, in the opinion of the Seanad, the Government should formulate a scheme of war risk insurance for property, and take the necessary steps to put the scheme into operation'.[33] In the earlier debate, Seán McEntee, the Minister for Industry and Commerce, promised to give consideration to this matter. The later debate centred on damage should Ireland be attacked, and what was actually said was that the question would arise only at the end of the war. The *Sunday Independent*, however, had now asked the question. The answer in the minds of the affected residents was clear and unambiguous: compensation would indeed be available.

The city manager and his chief architect accepted that repairs would be necessary, and seemed certain that recompense would flow from the government for all such repairs and restoration. Those repairs, as well as the manifold various other demands for compensation sought by the affected residents, are the main topic of this work.

THE INITIAL RESPONSE OF THE CORPORATION

Not alone did the rescue services respond to the incident quickly; so too did the city architect. On 3 January, the day of the earlier Terenure bombing, a conference of officials was summoned by the city manager and O'Rourke was instructed to take complete charge of demolition and repair operations.[34] The following day O'Rourke appointed five contractors to the two areas bombed: Terenure and Donore Terrace (which was in the Rialto area of Dublin City for these purposes). These were the depot contractors who had already worked on the rescue and demolition service programme with the Corporation. They were explicitly appointed to deal only with repairs of residential property; repairs on public buildings, churches and halls were to be dealt with by contractors appointed by the owners. And they were to concern themselves only with bomb repair damage; no demolished residential property was to be dealt with by them. O'Rourke also got four of the Corporation's own building surveyors to survey the affected areas on that Friday, and to record in detail the conditions of all property.

On the same day, Hernon had a meeting with Seán Moylan, parliamentary secretary to the Minister for Industry and Commerce. Moylan expressed satisfaction with the speedy response by the Corporation, and went on to say that he had little doubt that the state would have to pay back all the damage incurred, but that they would rely on the Corporation to see that the charges were reasonable.[35]

Still on 4 January, O'Rourke made a confident report to Hernon in which he proposed that 'repairs to all residential property will be carried out by the Corporation contractors, half-a-dozen [actually five] of whom have already been nominated to carry out this work'. By this stage he was probably unaware that the residents had already begun to take matters into their own hands. O'Rourke also appointed private quantity surveyors for each of the areas affected to check and value the work of all the contractors, official and private.[36] The stated reason was because there were not sufficient of the Corporation's own staff to undertake the work.

Two days later O'Rourke wrote to Hernon drawing attention to his memo of 7 October 1940.[37] As well as reiterating his earlier request for a 'rescue and demolition' service, he added the additional point – the government should be requested at once to introduce emergency legislation to cover the local authority's responsibility for compensation. The contractors submitted a joint letter on 8 January setting out the terms they required. O'Rourke recommended their acceptance, and proposed that those same terms would also be applicable to all future contractors, so that subsequent operations could be started immediately 'on a cut-and-dry basis without delay or negotiation'.[38] In his letter of 9 January detailing all this, O'Rourke considered cases of complete rebuilding and recommended that such work should be carried out by the owners, who would then submit claims which would be subject to valuation and, if necessary, arbitration. It would be a condition that the work would be awarded based on a competitive tender. Hernon's response was to tell O'Rourke to carry out repairs with 'as much rapidity as possible'.[39] Eight days later, in a memorandum of 17 January, O'Rourke clarified matters both for the two bombings and for future events. He had approached the bodies representing (he says 'controlling') contractors and quantity surveyors to ensure they were aware of his views.[40] He also proposed, as he had done the previous October, the formation of a special repair branch. He strongly recommended that a clerk of works should be appointed for each area 'to prevent partially idle working staffs or damage unnecessarily increased for which the Corporation would be asked to pay … Also bogus claims could be investigated in the early stages'. Then, ominously, he continued 'If this provision is neglected there may be trouble in case of a local government audit following a prolonged interval'.

As an indication of what was to follow, O'Rourke gloomily reported that the scope of repairs 'is and will present great difficulty in limitation, as claims are coming in for damage to garden structures and shrubs, garages and tool sheds, seats, etc., and contractors are prone to cover all details as the Corporation is deemed to be responsible … It may be noted that many claimants could afford reinstatement at their own expense'.

On 23 January O'Rourke made his first estimation of the cost of repairing the damage. He informed the city manager that the total cost of rebuilding demolished residential properties and repairing institutional buildings was likely to exceed £5,000, and a total approximate liability might be in the region of £30,000. He recommended that a fund of £250,000 be available to cover this and all subsequent damage in the central Dublin area.[41] O'Rourke's assessment of the quality of building in the houses affected was not high, declaring that almost all the property affected was of 'speculative builders' standard', and therefore easily damaged.

It was already clear that O'Rourke's plans were not being followed by the residents. A week later, on 31 January, he reported that, in addition to the three contractors appointed to work in the Donore area, private contractors entered the areas on orders from property owners, and were being allowed to proceed on the same basis of payment as those who were appointed officially. What he calls a 'mass of correspondence' had already been received from owners, and more worryingly, 'their advisers'. Their demands were quite explicit, but the Corporation had not yet had a reply from the Department of Defence, which was dealing with the claims on behalf of the Government. Reporting that some demands for clear undertakings had been replied to 'in an evasive manner', he now felt that at least two months would elapse before a complete picture of the destruction would appear. In addition, the bitterly cold weather of that January already meant that four of the 20 working days since the bombing had been lost, and delay was 'likely to continue'.[42]

As further evidence of the residents' recognition of the possibilities of compensation, claims were already coming in for re-decoration, clearly contrary to his instructions, but with private contractors working on the jobs, this was proving difficult to control. Already a 'small number' of claims had been received that O'Rourke considered 'obviously non bona-fide'. He acknowledges that the 'complete attention' necessary would prolong the repair works 'indefinitely'.[43]

Nor was it alone the residents who were now attempting to frustrate O'Rourke's plans. The contractors had adopted the method of spreading out labour on the largest number of premises, to hold as much as possible of the work, and this prevented rapid completion, but this practice impressed occupiers that their claims were receiving attention.

During this initial period, O'Rourke still found time to plan for future possible bombings. In correspondence with Hernon on 9, 17 and 23 January he expressly stated the need to change procedures and give extra necessary authorization to cover 'further potential incidents' and in order that operations might start, as he said, automatically.[44]

On 30 January, nearly a month after the incident, the Government finally issued a memorandum detailing the procedures to be followed by any Local Authority seeking compensation payments for bombing of any sort. This was memorandum H.2725/2/41, issued by 'J(ames) Hurson, Rúnaí (Secretary)' on behalf of the Minister for Local Government and Public Health.[45] In it the minister specified how payments to contractors employed in making good the damage caused by bombing in Donore Terrace were to be made, and what arrangements were authorized in regard to the carrying out of repairs together with the provision of clothing and furniture as well as alternative accommodation. Firstly, all expenditure incurred was to be recouped by the local authority by way of an advance out of monies provided by the Oireachtas. When the Corporation had received the accounts and were satisfied in regard to the amount, the payment should be defrayed by the Corporation. The following arrangements were the authorized ones:

> Immediately after the occurrence, the appropriate technical officer would visit the area, assess the damage, and estimate the cost of repairs.

> Where damage prevented the house being used for accommodation, the responsibility for repair would rest with the Corporation unless the occupier took it upon themselves. The cost should be less than £100, unless the Corporation were satisfied that this was insufficient, where up to £130 might be made.

> Where a house has been destroyed, and the income of the householder is less than £400 per annum, advances of up to £30 for clothing and £50 for replacement furniture if the temporary accommodation is unfurnished.

Any such advances to be deducted from compensation 'ultimately payable'.

In his final correspondence in this initial period after the bombing, O'Rourke with 'regret' troubled the city manager with a memorandum on 5 February.[46] There was still no clear authority under which he might proceed. The surveyors (who were appointed to relieve the Corporation's own staff) as well as the contractors were looking to the Corporation to resolve all problems of negotiation with owners. Repairs, including stained glass and garden seats, were being carried out by the contractors, and control of this practice was proving difficult.

Covering any future incidents, O'Rourke announced the appointment of contractors and quantity surveyors for the nine remaining unaffected Dublin city areas. He now recognized that an essential part of any future plan would be greatly increased supervision – it was a clear condition in the memorandum from the Department of Local Government on such work, requiring from the outset the estimated cost of making good the damage. Additionally, the maximum sanctionable expenditure allowed for in that memorandum of £130 per premises struck O'Rourke as being unreasonable; or, as he put it, it was not clear how it was arrived at. He finally recommended that in any future incidents the Corporation should be responsible only for the initial survey by its own officers, and to check on subsequent independent claims invited by press advertisement from property owners who would carry out permanent repairs themselves. In a memorandum to the city manager on 29 January, O'Rourke detailed the damage: two houses (91 and 93) completely demolished and 22 where the residents had been forced to seek alternative accommodation.[47] In addition, 520 houses were 'injured but not vacated'. By the date of this memorandum, 173 were 'already dealt with'.

In a report compiled by the official contractors on 11 February, and sent to Hurson on 18 January, detailed information on all the affected houses is given.[48] Thirteen houses on Donore Terrace – nos. 86 to 96 on the North side and 85 to 97 on the south – were described as the 'main job'. In addition, another 17 houses on the terrace had damage described as 'heavy' to 'very heavy'. A further 28 houses on the South Circular Road were damaged, four on Wolseley Street, four on Washington Street and three on Greenville Avenue. On Parnell Road 35 houses were damaged, and, since the canal forms one side of that road, all were on the south side, the side farthest from the bombing. All the houses on Arbutus Avenue, from Fitzpatrick's at no. 1 to Daly's at no. 20 were damaged, as were all six occupied houses on Parnell Avenue, and 11 of the 22 on Lullymore Terrace. Over half the houses on Dufferin Avenue (36 out of 64) were listed, along with 16 houses on Washington Street, 21 on Donore Avenue, three on St Alban's Avenue and two on Sandford Avenue.

The list already referred to of those displaced from the terrace, showing where they found alternative accommodation, also gives us information about their conditions and possible hints about the relationships within the houses.[49] Four went to friends, 15 stayed with relatives, ten rented accommodation and four were boarding or lodging.

In a 'Précis of operations' drawn up by O'Rourke on 18 February, the city architect described the chain of events:

3/1/1941   City manager informed by chief warden about 4 a.m.

City manager summoned a conference of technical officials and instructed the city architect to prepare a programme of repair operations.

City architect submitted the foregoing which were verbally approved by the city manager 4/1/1941

4/1/1941   City architect instructed three building surveyors and one inspector of dangerous buildings to make a survey of the area and record all visible damage.

City architect appointed by letter five building contractors as official contractors (two for Rathdown and three for Rialto areas) with verbal approval of city manager. City architect also appointed by letter two quantity surveyors.

6/1/1941   City architect reported in detail to city manager his further recommendations regarding procedure in the programme submitted from inspections made in the areas.

9/1/1941   Two architectural assistants appointed to supervise contractors.

City architect reported in detail to city manager terms of payment for official contractors, and requested official sanction.

City architect received verbal instructions from city manager that private contractors employed by property owners should be allowed to operate also.[50]

To summarize: the Corporation, through the city manager and city architect, had moved with commendable speed to set up procedures for repairing damaged residential property, involving official contractors and quantity surveyors, and with clear instructions that the only repairs to be undertaken were those sufficient merely to render the house habitable. Demolished houses were not to be rebuilt, work was to be restricted to dwelling houses, and no redecoration was to be done. The government had indicated that it might be more generous in this area, but no clear instructions had been received. All had been done within eight days of the bombing. With the infrastructure in place, and the procedures agreed, O'Rourke was now in a position to manage the job of repairing – making re-inhabitable – the dwellings damaged by the bombs of 4 January.

3. Repairing, redecorating, recriminations

If the Corporation had moved swiftly, so too had the residents. While, as mentioned earlier, O'Rourke was confidently reporting to Hernon on 4 January that repairs to all residential property would be carried out by the official Corporation contractors, unofficial contractors appear, from newspaper reports and photographs, to have begun working on damaged houses on that very Saturday, the day after the bombing; indeed, in an unsigned handwritten note of 3 January – to repeat, the very day of the bombing – possibly from Mr H.G. Simms, housing architect, O'Rourke was explicitly told that the assistant city architect, Conor McGinley, had phoned the writer of the note to inform him that that some owners had 'already made independent arrangements with private contractors to carry out repairs', and the contractors' men were already 'on the ground'.[1] McGinley, not unsurprisingly, requested 'direction', and he wanted it quickly – he stated that he would ring from Donore Terrace that afternoon, although how he proposed doing this (in days of very limited telephone coverage) was not stated.

Matters were moving more quickly than O'Rourke might have liked; in a memorandum to Hernon, still on the Friday of the bombing, he confirmed that salvage had already become a matter of difficulty as occupiers insisted on removing their goods, 'but I have informed them that owner removal will preclude any compensation claim in the future'.[2]

Finally, on what had been a most busy Friday, O'Rourke officially informed the three contractors assigned to the Rialto district of their appointment. They were: W. & J. Bolger, J. Fearon, and G.P. Walsh.[3]

In less than a week, O'Rourke's self-confidence had reasserted itself, and he wrote to Hernon on 10 January telling him that works were 'now in full swing by official contractors and private contractors after many difficulties of procedure have been surmounted. Notifications of damage were coming in daily'.[4] Nonetheless, he pointed out rather primly that some contractors were acting 'in an independent manner which cannot be recognized later'. And some claims he noted were 'not apparently bona fide', and may have referred to 'neglected or decayed property'.

By this stage, over three weeks after the bombing, the contractors were submitting bills and the Corporation was looking for money from the Department. On 28 January Hurson wrote to Hernon that the matter of payment for making good damage to houses at Donore Terrace was 'receiving attention'.[5] On 1 February, O'Rourke was able to report to Hernon that the

5 Destroyed house

rate of progress of repairs had been reasonable, 'but of course it could not satisfy everyone. I also consider that there is nothing to fear from reasonable criticism'.[6]

Three weeks later a new element was introduced. On 20 February Hernon wrote to Hurson referring to letters he had received from solicitors on behalf of clients seeking compensation for loss of rent, personal injuries and consequential losses.[7] Hernon's response was precise: the department had not authorized him to make such payments, and he took it for granted, therefore, that all correspondence should be forwarded to the department. In letters the same day he informed the applicants (and not their solicitors) of this.

The Corporation's room for manoeuvre had, however, been compromised both by the speed of response by the residents and the behaviour of neighbouring authorities, for on 27 February Moylan discussed matters with the Corporation.[8] He informed them that Dún Laoghaire Corporation had already paid for decorations in the Sandycove area after the bombing there in December 1940, and, furthermore, that the terms of the general memorandum of 30 January could not be applied in Donore, as *ad hoc* instructions had already been given in these cases before the terms of that memorandum were settled. In other words, it was up to the Corporation to deal with claims themselves.

The residents were now getting bolder, and, on 13 March, O'Rourke wrote to Hernon telling him that the matters of greatest difficulty were roofs and ceilings, where weather damage could not be easily separated from bomb damage, and the condition of old and neglected ceilings were being rendered worse from day to day by 'means open to suspicion on the part of occupiers or contractors'. The situation had, O'Rourke continued, been greatly aggravated by the persistence of new claims and the formation of a local committee to advance claims already made.

This was the Donore Terrace (bombed damage) area committee, ably led by Senator Margaret Kennedy of no. 117. Senator Miss Margaret Kennedy was a formidable woman. On 31 March 1938 Éamon de Valera nominated 11 individuals to Seanad Éireann, as he was required to do by the new constitution. Margaret L. Kennedy was one of these. In the Taoiseach's own words:

> She was the only person rightfully holding the rank of Commandant in the Cumann na mBan organization, responsible as Commandant for all branches in city and part of the County for that period, the most troublesome and active period of the Black and Tan War. During the Truce she spent two months organizing Sinn Féin Clubs in Sligo and establishing lines of communication. In June 1922 she was about to go north under orders when hostilities again broke out and she set up a hospital for the O'Connell Street area ... she was the first woman for whom a warrant of arrest was issued in 1922.[9]

On 28 February the secretary of the association, John Brown, wrote to Hernon inquiring as to the situation in regards to painting and decorating.[10] He told the city manager that Seán T. O'Kelly, the Minister for Finance, had informed the Senator that houses would have to be made 'fit for habitation again, [and] that they should be painted etc.'.[11]

On 18 July the senator wrote to de Valera, beginning her letter with 'a chara' – 'friend'.[12] She drew his attention to a few points that appeared not to be definitely covered by the proposed Act. These included:

> The painting and decorating of the house
> Removal and storage of furniture
> Alternative accommodation
> Replacement of outbuildings (garages etc.)
> Destruction of motor cars

and the committee declared that they would be glad if the Taoiseach either raised these points, or supported them if already brought forward.

The senator obviously had telephone conversations with her old friend, for in a memorandum from the Taoiseach's Rúnaí Príobháideach (Private Secretary) dated 4 October 1941 to his opposite number for the Aire Airgeadais (Minister for Finance) reference is made to such communication.[13] Dev's 'understanding' was that Finance would deal directly with the senator, and then send him a copy of the report. Finance wrote to the senator on 13 October, beginning *their* letter with the much more formal A Bhean Uasal (best translated as Madam), and basically conceding almost everything.[14] Even the matter of rates, to be referred to below, was discussed – that matter would be passed on to the Minister for Local Government.

On 28 July the committee wrote to the city manager.[15] The vacated houses were still uninhabitable, and on behalf of 18 of the residents who had been unable to return to their homes, they asked him to either get a remission of the rates for the period or get the Minister for Local Government and Public Health to 'make arrangements'. Ominously, the footnote to the letter stated 'any reply may be sent to Senator Miss Kennedy, 117 Donore Terrace'.

Hernon himself was by now clearly aware of the exposure of the Corporation to such claims, for some months earlier on 22 March he wrote to the Department informing them that it was, in his words, quite obvious that limiting work to repairs necessary to permit the premises to be occupied did not satisfy the demands of the 'victims of the bombings'.[16] He had received many letters and a daily quota of callers who had pointed out that redecorating and painting were necessary, and that they were financially unable to undertake such work. In a very large number of the damaged houses, the occupiers were dependent wholly or partially on the letting of rooms for their livelihood, and it was quite apparent that rooms in which the contractors had been making repairs had been left in an unlettable condition. He also pointed out, however, that the houses, particularly those in the Donore Terrace area, were all old, and had received 'but little internal attention' during the previous few years. He now felt that 'at least a limited amount of decoration' could be carried out as part of the general repair scheme.

The political pressure from TDs, including ministers, was also becoming evident, and Moylan wrote firstly to the city manager on 8 April giving him discretion to accept claims without asking for ministerial approval, and then on 10 April asking the manager for 'some little redecorative work' to be done on the house of one of his own [Moylan's] staff.[17] He continued 'while our official minute … deals with re-decorative work in cases of hardship, I do not think it should be interpreted too literally'.

O'Rourke's response was characteristically blunt: such claims should not be entertained, and he had declined to sanction it. On 16 April he wrote to Hernon stating that 'so far only one case claimed as hardship has come to my notice, but all occupiers, including well-to-do owners, claim hardship'.

Whatever the Minister might suggest, O'Rourke stated that it was very difficult to decide what was 'essential redecorative work', or to carry out work 'with discretion' in face of the active pursuit of parties interested. Furthermore, he explained why redecoration was not being covered. This was primarily because the bombing was being used to redecorate 'where their landlords had neglected the premises for long periods previously'. In addition, the occupiers were by that stage 'organized to watch the scope of repairs and secure that what is done in one premises shall be done in every other'. He would 'be obliged for a direction'. He was at this stage conscious of the precedents being set by the de-facto situation as it was evolving in Donore. In a typed postscript he stated that he had been for some weeks very anxious to close down 'this scheme of repairs' in view of his belief that similar circumstances might arise 'any day again', and, should the Donore scheme still be current, the Corporation's room for manoeuvre would be severely limited.[18]

On 30 April O'Rourke wrote to the three official contractors complaining the works of repairs were being unnecessarily prolonged, and that if the progress were not considerably speeded up, he would make an order postponing the issue of any further instalments of payments.[19] However in a handwritten note in the copy he sent to the city manager, he pointed out that 'the answer of these contractors may well be that as claims are being entertained indefinitely and the work constantly added to they cannot be expected to complete'.

Finally, on 1 May, O'Rourke capitulated.[20] He wrote to Hernon stating 'it has been decided that an allowance in cash of £5 per habitable room would be paid to the property owner (underlined in original) to enable the owner to have any general renewal done by any decoration contractor'. By then a significant amount of the rebuilding and renovation had been completed. Detailed reports are, not unsurprisingly, only available from the official contractors, but E. O'Byrne of the city architect's department made a series of 'progress reports' which were sent to the ARP section for Hernon's attention.[21]

On 22 February, in addition to five houses owned by the Corporation and dealt with separately by the Corporation Housing Maintenance section and the two demolished properties, repairs were complete on 68 houses, 'progressing' on 188, and 347 were still to be dealt with – a total of 610. On 8 March the figures were 251 complete, 216 progressing and 148 still to be dealt with. With the other seven houses, that came to 622. The typewritten note to the report commented that the figure was increasing as belated reports came to hand and were investigated. In a rather frantic handwritten note (in his characteristic red ink) O'Rourke notes the increase. The following week, the total was 644 and O'Rourke commented again. A week later the figure was 649, on 29 March 652, and the total in the final report of 21 June was 668 without the Corporation houses, or 673 in all. While a total of 63 houses had reported damage more than five weeks after the bombs fell, in 654 of the 668 houses, work was complete.

Somewhat precise distinctions were being made by Hernon. One of the terrace residents, seeing her neighbour's stables being rebuilt, asked about her own greenhouse. Hernon told her, regretfully, that while he was repairing permanent structures such as stables and garages, temporary ones, such as greenhouses, were excluded. As a fine example of lateral thinking, the affected resident reminded Hernon that no less a personage than the President had 'repeatedly and urgently' advised citizens to grow all the food possible, and, for this, obviously, a greenhouse was necessary.[22] The actual repair work was, just four months after the incident, now coming to an end. The Corporation wrote to nos. 91 and 93, the two demolished houses, on 9 May stating that demolition work was complete, and they should make their own arrangements in regard to the 'cleared site', asking them to retake possession no later than 16 May.[23]

It now became a matter of seeing who would take responsibility for paying the contractors. On 29 May O'Rourke wrote to Hernon seeking authority to pay all outstanding repair claims by the 'unofficial' contractors.[24] Hernon annotated the note by hand 'subject to Minister's sanction', and, on 10 June (a long delay by Hernon's standard) wrote to Hurson, basically doing a simple re-write of O'Rourke's letter, and seeking Ministerial authorization. In a reply dated 23 July (again a long delay), the Minister authorized repairs up to £130 (the original £100 limit 'in all but exceptional cases' had by now been dropped completely) and going on to say that even this larger figure might be exceeded 'by a few pounds', and 'some reasonable flexibility allowed'.[25] Criteria for this discretion were not given, but Hernon was reminded that matters had been discussed 'over the 'phone' the previous month and the Corporation officials had the position 'explained to them'.

It was additionally becoming clear that it was going to be difficult to apportion costs to individual houses. Whether by agreement or independently, many of the contractors grouped the houses on which they were working and submitting total claims without any individual breakdown. Nos. 57 and 58 Dufferin Avenue, for instance, were submitted together. In addition, they also did not limit themselves to the £130 limit proposed by O'Rourke; the repairs on 115 Donore Terrace, for instance, cost £220 17s. 9d. The official contractors proved no better; in his letter to the city architect on 26 July, Thomas C. Whelan, quantity surveyor, explicitly states that it was 'absolutely impossible to keep separate the cost of repairs in each premises'.

On 18 July Hernon wrote to Moylan stating that repairs for the bombing could not be individually vouched. Those terms were being followed in the North Strand, but 'as arrangements for repairing work had been completed before 30 January', Hernon took it that those accounts would have to be paid 'without requiring the individual cost in the case of each premises'.

On 25 June O'Rourke was able to tell Hernon that most of the work of the official contractors was finished, with only 11 houses still being repaired, and two where the owners were refusing access to the contractors. However, over 300 of these houses still had not been inspected, and, citing shortage of staff, the city architect was of the opinion that the work would take several months. He went on: 'I have consistently endeavoured to keep the scope [of the repairs] within reasonable limits, but it has proved to be a matter of great difficulty'. The demolition work and main rebuilding were complete. The job, however, was only half done.

REDECORATION

'Dear Sir, I would be obliged if you would get my house papered and painted, as the walls look very bad without paper or paint'.[26]

Having secured renovation to their premises, the residents now shifted attention to a wide variety of other claims.

Almost from the day of the bombing, it is clear that Hernon recognized the importance of non-structural damage, even to household effects, for on 7 January he wrote to William Montgomery & Son (Dublin), Valuers, 24 Suffolk Street, referring to the work of survey and valuation they were already carrying out on behalf of the Corporation in the affected areas; on 10 January he wrote an internal memorandum confirming their appointment to Mr Fagan, of the Office of Public Works.[27] The next day Montgomerys began sending reports of 'damaged effects' to the city manager, including the actual cost of repairing the damage to furniture, the cost of cleaning and shaking carpets, the cost of laundering, and the fair market value of items destroyed. The claim explicitly excluded cash and jewellery; Hernon forwarded the reports to Hurson and Fagan.[28]

On 13 January a public notice appeared in the newspapers in which the Government indicated that it was prepared to compensate those who suffered damage as a result of such bombing. It read:

Compensation for War Damage

Where the origin of the bombs or other weapons of aerial attack, dropped on this country can be established, the external Government concerned has been or will be asked to accept liability for the loss and damage sustained and to pay compensation accordingly.

Pending the outcome of such representations, the Irish Government, acting through the appropriate local authority takes responsibility for making good the damage and relieving distress, subject to such conditions and restrictions as will be announced later.[29]

Montgomerys sent reports to Hernon throughout January and the beginning of February 1941. The amount estimated varied enormously, and not all differences can be readily explained.[30]

No. 91, Day's, one of the demolished pair, suffered by far the most serious damage, with £446 11s. 6d. for the family themselves, and £15 15s. 0d. for Lucy Reddy who also lived there. The Roiths, the owners of the other house destroyed, claimed less than a quarter of this amount: £91 13s. 6d.

The damage to the houses at the western end of the terrace may be indicative of the different approaches to injury suffered. The contractors reported the damage to nos. 116, 118 and 119 as being 'heavy'.[31] Yet all three houses are listed as having suffered no damage whatever to furniture or other effects. And although all of houses on the terrace, as stated earlier, were shown as having suffered structural damage that was either 'heavy' or 'very heavy', it was only the houses immediately adjoining the two destroyed where the damage to goods exceeded £100 – nos. 85, 87, 89, 95 and 97.

There is certainly evidence that claimants were slow in both realizing and applying for their entitlements. Beginning in that same set of reports of 8 January, Montgomerys were continually listing more and more houses that 'previously reported no damage but now advise some damage to effects'. In one case, for instance, inspectors called twice to a premises only to be informed by the housekeeper on both occasions that no damage had been suffered. Nearly a month later, however, the owner claimed for medicines that were damaged, equipment that had become rusty and a broken lamp bulb.[32] He was unable to provide details of the medicines, but asserted in February that the amount claimed, £30, was an under-estimate.[33] The workshop that replaced the lamp bulb stated that no bulb had been in the lamp – the gentleman said it had been thrown out. The equipment had been left in the open for the month – a month of some particularly bad weather. Another claim was for 'a valuable oil painting by an eminent Italian artist'.[34] Neither artist nor subject were recalled. In a third claim, the loss of ten years work in translating terms and phrases into Irish was described by the compiler as being 'incalculable', and he claimed 'only' the 'nominal' sum of £100.[35]

Montgomerys final report was sent to Hernon on 19 February. They were in a position to estimate the total for damage to contents in the Rialto area. Allowing for the absence of information on houses in which a considerable amount of furniture had been totally destroyed, and for which they had still to receive details, the total amount was assessed as:

Parnell Road	£247 14s. 6d.
Dufferin Avenue	£110 5s. 6d.
SCR	£2,559 6s. 5d.
Total	£2,917 6s. 5d.

Apart from the terrace itself, only one house in the area had estimated damage to goods of over £100, a house in Parnell Road where the damage, initially estimated at £140 15s. 6d., was assessed as £101 1s. 6d.[36]

It seems, to say the least, to have been uncomfortable for O'Rourke that Montgomerys, on behalf of Hernon, were visiting the affected properties and taking details of damages to contents whilst his own contractors and quantity surveyors were assessing and repairing damaged properties, and refusing to entertain any claim for contents. Additionally, in contrast to the imprecise nature of the claims with which O'Rourke was dealing, with no real breakdown of costs and several properties often grouped together in a single bill, Montgomerys listed each house separately, said what was examined and, if not on the relevant premises, *where* it was examined.[37]

As to the actual process of compensation, an exchange in the Dáil between Deputy Henry Dockrell, Deputy Alfred Byrne and the Minister for Finance in the Dáil on 5 February 1941 clarified matters still further:

> **Mr Byrne** asked the Minister for Finance if he is in a position to state if the Government propose to compensate those who suffered loss as a result of the recent bombings.

> **Mr Dockrell** asked the Minister for Finance whether, in view of the recent air raids, there is any fund available from which compensation to life or property can be made; whether the question of compensation depends on the responsible country acknowledging liability, and agreeing to pay for the injury caused by air raids; whether, also, damage to decoration, electrical wiring, fittings, carpets, linoleum and furniture is included in the compensation referred to in the recent Government statement.

> **Mr Ó Ceallaigh** I propose to answer Questions 3 and 4 together. I would refer the Deputies to the public notice issued on 11th January 1941, that the Government takes responsibility for making good the damage caused by the recent dropping of bombs on this country. That responsibility is assumed irrespective of the outcome of representations to any external Government. In due course, the Dáil will be asked to make the necessary financial provision. Conditions and procedure have yet to be settled but, probably, such items as those mentioned by deputy Dockrell will be covered.[38]

Deputy Dockrell, who represented Dublin County in the Dáil, seems to have been primed; his question concerning 'damage to decoration, electrical wiring, fittings, carpets, linoleum and furniture' were all items on Hernon's lists.

Almost immediately claims began coming in anticipating the legislation, and, in response, Hernon wrote a standard letter to affected individual householders:

> In reply to your letter claiming compensation for damage by bombs at the above premises, I would inform you that the Minister for Finance in Dáil Éireann on the 5 February 1941, indicated that legislation is contemplated to deal with claims for damage caused by bombing incidents. No announcement as to the types of claim to be considered or the procedure to be followed in making such claims, or the basis of assessing payment can be made in anticipation of the publication of the Bill. I am consequently returning your estimate, and would advise you to await the promised legislation before making your claim.[39]

Finally, just over six months after the bombing, on 8 July 1941, the Minister for Finance asked the Dáil for

> leave to introduce a Bill entitled an Act to make provision for the payment of compensation out of public moneys to persons who, on or after the 26th day of August, 1940, suffer injury to their property in the State or the territorial waters thereof as a consequence of an act of the armed forces of an external Government or authority engaged in a war in respect of which the State is neutral or as a consequence of an accidental occurrence arising from something done outside the State by any such armed force, and to make provision for matters connected with such injuries to property or the payment of compensation therefor.[40]

The Neutrality (War Damage to Property) Act, 1941 (No. 24/1941) was enacted on 23 September, and Section 17 of the Act described the relationship between the Department and the Local Authority and the Corporation:

> 17. (1) Whenever a building has suffered (whether before or after the passing of this Act) an injury to which this Act applies, the following provisions shall apply and have effect, that is to say:
> (a) it shall be lawful for the local authority in whose functional area such building is situate to enter on such building and there do all such things as shall be necessary for the purpose of ascertaining the nature and extent of such injury.

Essentially, the Corporation was indemnified for all its costs, for all its work and for all previous bombings. The wisdom of Hernon's appointment of Montgomerys now became clear, for their careful itemizing of damages could now be contrasted with the rather haphazard costings of O'Rourke, his contractors and his quantity surveyors. For them, compliance with memorandum H.2725/2/41 would soon become an issue.

RECRIMINATIONS

The issue now became the contentious one of finding out who was to blame for the chaos that was the compensation claim for structural repair for the January bombing. The memorandum of 31 January was clear: the Corporation would repair the buildings and these costs would be recouped. The control of these costs was explicitly referred to by O'Rourke at a conference on 14 February.[41] The city architect complained that the affair was proving a gold-mine for all the contractors involved, and that it was impossible to monitor their work. Hernon made several suggestions, all of which presented O'Rourke with difficulties, but he promised to think over the matter and present the city manager with a scheme within 24 hours. His response, dated 17 February, basically said that the scheme was unworkable and should, even at that stage, be discontinued.[42] His recommendation was for an unspecific 'alternative'.

The problems became far more concrete in late summer of 1941 when Seán Ó Suilleabháin, city accountant, became involved. In a letter to J.P. Keane, principal officer of the Finance Section of Dublin Corporation dated 8 July, he asked explicitly for individual detailed expenses for each house, and, in a follow-up letter on 10 July, noted that one of the quantity surveyors had given three items on a bill – two individual houses and a further four grouped together – and suggested that it seemed possible to further segregate those four.[43]

Although O'Rourke was not mentioned in this correspondence, perhaps seeing what way the wind was blowing he wrote to Hernon on 18 July, begging leave to submit comments.[44] O'Rourke reminded Hernon that, firstly, the main memo from the Minister (H2725/2/41) arrived a full month after work had started, and he had raised these issues both at the time and subsequently. Secondly, given the January weather, he could not afford to wait until an estimate had been made of the cost each individual repair. While the official contractors had done no redecoration (or rather, they had employed no painters or decorators), this was not so for the unofficial contractors. Finally, there were cases where the cost of *necessary* work exceeded the £130 limit. As so frequently in the past, he 'awaited instructions'. The problems experienced by O'Rourke in complying with the January memo, however, continued unabated. Just three days later, on 21 July, Moylan was still asking Hernon that an effort be made to apportion the costs of each house.[45]

On 17 September 1941 O'Rourke wrote to Hernon stating that the quantity surveyors, whose job it was to certify the work done by the

contractors – official and unofficial – could provide such figures only with
difficulty; the same problems arose with the fees of the quantity surveyors
themselves.[46] Moylan had written to Hernon on 24 July asking him to be
'good enough' to explain on what terms as regards remuneration he had
employed quantity surveyors.[47] Hernon forwarded the letter the next day to
O'Rourke, asking for the necessary information. O'Rourke's reply, on the
same day, quoted from the letters of appointment: the 'usual surveyor's fees'
would be payable, and, still on 25 July, Hernon replied to the secretary,
including with the letter a bill from one of the surveyors, Thomas C. Whelan.
Pointing out that the fees seemed rather high, he asked Moylan to raise the
matter with the Minister so as to consider whether it was reasonable to
continue with the agreed basis of payment, adding, in a sign that he was
beginning to appreciate the danger to his own position, 'the city architect's
report does not help in the solution of the matter'. In a letter to R.S. Lawrie,
chief warden in the Air Raid Precaution Department of the Corporation
(whose name he misspells), Moylan asked in a most courteous fashion for
similar information on the North Strand bombings, adding, so as to ensure
that it would not be seen as aggressive, the comment 'this is a personal letter'.
Interestingly, the letter was filed, presumably with the city manager's
knowledge, in the Donore file.[48]

On 4 September the Department answered Hernon, stating that the
Minister would be unable to recommend recoupment on that scale. The
Secretary finished by firstly conceding that the city architect had no means of
checking time spent – the fundamental basis for payment – but that, given the
facts, the Minister proposed that Hernon agree to pay the quantity surveyors
a percentage ('say 5 per cent') of the total repair costs.[49]

On 20 December the city manager wrote to O'Rourke asking that he be
informed of the headings under which the quantity surveyors had been
employed in the area for which the city architect was responsible.[50] O'Rourke
was asked what checks he had applied towards ensuring that the surveyors
only did the work they were contracted to do, and what checks he had taken
and was taking to have evidence available for checking their accounts when
submitted. Hernon asked that the matter be given early attention. He got his
reply on 22 December. Everything had been done properly and there was no
extraneous work.[51]

The contractors were no better. In December George Fagan of the OPW
wrote to Hernon asking for full vouchers from the householders, and Keane
(now deputy city manager) passed on the letter to O'Rourke, blithely asking
O'Rourke whether a reply could be sent to Mr Fagan informing him that the
city architect would be in a position to facilitate the OPW.[52] O'Rourke
replied – with obvious exasperation shown by his use of red underlining –
pointing out that the official contractors worked under the direction of his

office, and the owners themselves had no relevant knowledge and could therefore provide no information on that work.[53] Finally, in February 1942, O'Rourke wrote with some concern to Keane that the contractors had *still* not been paid for work done the previous summer.[54] Keane forwarded the letter to Moylan, who, being in the Department of Health and Local Government and Public Health, should not have been privy to the correspondence, asking could the balances be paid, and adding 'I am sending this to you unofficially, so please return at your convenience'. The following month Moylan wrote to Hernon conceding, in the end, that the Departments involved, in view of the Corporation's difficulty in segregating the work done, had 'perforce' to be content with the arrangement.[55] But even as late as 9 May 1942 he was writing again to the city manager telling him that it was O'Rourke's responsibility to justify any departure from the by now accepted 'rule' that payments would be sanctioned only for individual houses.[56]

In the end the residents got what they wanted. Houses were repaired and rendered habitable in spite of the fact that, in far too many cases, and contrary to an official requirement, nobody – not the residents, nor the contractors, nor the quantity surveyors – provided anything resembling a detailed and itemized breakdown of the costs of all this. This contrasted with the compensation paid for other damages under the 1941 Act, where fully itemized lists were available. Ominously, more and more it looked as if the person to be held responsible for any serious criticism of the Corporation was the city architect, Horace Tennyson O'Rourke.

4. The folklore

A surprisingly common thread in all narratives concerning the bombing is the Jewish nature of the areas and individuals affected. Indeed, the Dublin City Council index record of the relevant file states baldly that the areas affected were 'districts where many Jewish families resided', and, writing in 1999, Eunan O'Halpin states (without providing sources) that 'the far-fetched claim that the South Circular Road area was singled out for bombing in 1940 because it was Dublin's Jewish quarter, still has its adherents'.[1]

This thread is regularly found in the few documented oral histories of the war. For instance, David Read, in an interview conducted in 2005 as part of the BBC World War II archive *WW2 People's War*, asked Mick Synnott (who served in the RAF after the war) if he felt that the German bombing of Dublin was deliberate:

> They reckon – some say it was deliberate, some say it was accidental. Again, you're talking about the south sector and there was a big Jewish community there. A big Jewish community, and they were bombed. The synagogue was apparently bombed and damaged. When they were sorting the place out after the bombing, they found no end of loot, tea and so on. Because tea was rationed in them days, very much so. And they found all this tea in the synagogue. Apparently the Jews were holding it up, and it was sold apparently on the black market. That's how it was in them days. And again, there was an awful lot of anti-Jewish policy in Dublin in them days.[2]

In the same programme, Michael Kearney speculates that:

> Amiens Street station was bombed, because they were going up from Amiens Street Station in their thousands … we all believed the two reasons. First of all the Jews – that was deliberate. And Amiens Street station was deliberate. [errors in transcription corrected]

Similarly, in Maureen Diskin's contribution to Benjamin Grob-Fitzgibbon's oral history of WWII (recorded in April 2000) she recalls:

> But I do remember they also bombed a place called the South Circular Road, which, by a strange coincidence, was a Jewish stronghold. All the

6 Bombed synagogue

Jews in Dublin lived around the South Circular Road. All around there. An awful lot of Jews lived on the South Circular Road, and funnily enough that was where the Germans dropped the bomb, to try and hit their synagogue. They nearly hit their synagogue on the South Circular Road. But I was in bed that night and it lifted me out of my sheets. I remember that quite clearly.[3]

Nick Harris grew up in a Jewish household in the area; his birthplace, Greenville Terrace, was one of the streets most affected, and yet he makes no reference to the bombing. This is all the more unusual because his *schul*, Greenville Hall Synagogue, was the one damaged in the attack – the one Maureen Diskin suggested was 'targeted'.[4]

This paucity of reference in the more 'anecdotal' local histories is almost enough to stimulate curiosity as to its omission. Although Billy French has a chapter on the emergency in his *Memories of Crumlin*, and his father joined the LSF (the Local Security Force), he makes no reference to the bombs.[5] Similarly, Seosamh Ó Broin, in his description of Kilmainham and Inchicore (at the end of the South Circular Road) has a short chapter on 'The Emergency years', but no mention is made of the bombing.[6] Only one of those contributing to

Irene Wilson Power's history of St Catherine's National School on Donore Avenue – literally around the corner from the bomb site – described the attack. Interestingly that contributor (Irene Hayes) mentioned an incident not referred to anywhere else: the Presbyterian School on Donore Terrace was damaged, and the children let off school, unlike her and her companions in St Catherine's.[7] Only in the Catherine Scuffil edited history of Dolphin's Barn does one find any real description: three short paragraphs and some photographs, one clearly showing the damage to the house beside the synagogue mentioned above.[8]

REMINISCENCES

After nearly 70 years, it is unsurprising that there are only a few still living in the area who remember the events of January 1941 with clarity. It was fortuitous that, through the kindness of four extremely generous individuals, three such different and complementary sets of memories were shared with the writer. This is not an oral history. Such an exercise would be much more extensive, and would be carried out using a methodology and approach specifically designed to that purpose. There have been such histories of the period. Benjamin Grob-Fitzgibbon's excellent *The Irish experience during the Second World War, an oral history* is such, and the BBC's *WW2 People's War* project, asking ordinary people to contribute their memories of World War II to a website between June 2003 and January 2006 resulted in an archive of 47,000 stories and 15,000 images, all available on-line.[9] What was done for this study was a simple mail drop into the houses remaining on the terrace itself, as well as requests to old neighbours active in the community and more general requests to acquaintances whose families had lived in Dublin during the period. All three approaches led to introductions, and the response was one of great generosity. The interviews were simply that – a call to their house (where I was made most welcome) and a conversation on the bombing and its aftermath, as well as general discussion of the period itself. Details of all three conversations were entered on computer immediately after the meeting.

Mr Paddy Culligan – Donore Road[10]
Mr Paddy Culligan lives, and has lived all his long life, in Donore Road, a few hundred metres from the bombing. In 1941 he and his brother were in the local ARP group, led by a Mr Coughlan. This group was responsible for part of an area that ran from James Street through Marrowbone Lane to Dolphin's Barn, and along the South Circular Road to Leonard's Corner. Apart from their duties in the event of an emergency, the main task of this group was to ascertain, for the entire area, the number and position of the fire hydrants and

gas pipes, and to draw up a list of all those living in each house in the area, together with their age, with a view to providing appropriate gas masks.

In the first days of January 1941 he distinctly remembers bombers wheeling overhead, and when in the early hours of 3 January he heard the explosions, he knew it was a bomb. He and his brother decided to go to the scene, and arrived there about 5 a.m. By that stage the soldiers and LDF from the nearby Griffith Barracks, together with the Garda, had cordoned off the area and were well into the rescue attempt. It was clear that these were the people in charge, and no particular demands were made of the Culligans. It should be noted however that Lawrie reported that when *he* arrived at the scene, about the same time, there were a large number of wardens on duty under the direction of area warden Hennessy and deputy warden McGuinness.[11] At this stage it would appear that all the injured requiring hospitalization had been taken away. The lack of direction experienced by the Culligans, who seemed to be the only ARP members of their group there, was exacerbated by the fact that Mr Coughlan, their group warden, was prevented from entering the terrace by the army/LDF barriers.

The process of finding survivors was made much easier for the authorities because they had the ARP house lists mentioned above, showing the names and ages of the inhabitants in every building. This meant that they were able quickly to determine who was in each house and verify that they were accounted for.

In spite of this, when the brothers noticed that the front wall of the Roith's had actually fallen out, and that they could see clearly into the bedroom, they saw a small crying male child in the room. Scrambling up the broken wall, they brought the boy to safety and gave him to an ambulance man. The sight that greeted the two ARP men was captured on an *Irish Press* photograph (fig. 7); one can actually see how the pair could clamber up the demolished front wall of the house.[12] They then went to their own places of work, but felt quite unwell about midday. They were sent to a doctor who diagnosed that they had inhaled gas, and should take the afternoon off – which they did.

Paddy was impressed with the efficiency of Mr Hennessy, the area warden. He regularly called emergency mobilizations. On one Sunday morning, the 'bomb' was beside St Theresa's Church on Donore Avenue. The manoeuvres required that people be stopped from approaching the site, but the people on this occasion were mass-goers. In his description of the efforts taken to deal with this situation, Paddy answered a question raised in the previous chapter: how telephone contact was maintained between the emergency services and, indeed, between Corporation employees. It was simple: they used public phones, 'phones on the street' as Paddy Culligan called them. They were expected to have in their pockets the small coins necessary for such calls.

He is critical of those who claim that the area was targeted because of the large Jewish population. He feels that the pilot was lost, and, in addition, may

7 Demolished house

have mistaken the sheen of the canal for open water, and attempted to drop his remaining bombs there. He did however offer an intriguing explanation of the rumour. Later in the war, he and his brother, along with their father, were listening to a radio broadcast of *Germany calling* by William Joyce, Lord Haw-Haw. On this occasion, Joyce expressly bragged that the Jews of Dublin had been bombed. There are no records of Joyce's broadcasts, and this fact is mentioned by no other sources. Nonetheless, it does provide an explanation for the story; in some ways it is not relevant what was said in that broadcast, as Joyce almost certainly did not state explicitly that Germany had directly targeted neutral Dublin – such a statement would have created a diplomatic storm. What was important was that listeners heard the words 'Jews', 'Dublin' and 'bomb' together, and made a connection.

As to the personal experience of damage, the ceiling of the Culligan house in Donore Road was cracked after the blast, but no serious damage seemed to have occurred. Nonetheless, about 18 months later, the ceiling collapsed. It was quickly fixed by the contractors, who did not delay, and the costs were met by the Corporation. Paddy Culligan was emphatic that no spurious or excessive claims were made 'by anyone around here', and this is borne out by the official record.

Mr Jack Earley – South Circular Road[13]

Jack Earley still lives in the house to which his family moved in the late 1930s. The Earley house is a few metres east from Donore Terrace, opposite the National Stadium and the old barracks, now a private college. There were two parents and five children in the house, and the family ran a firm of stained glass manufacturers and a religious statuary works with office and workshops in Dublin's Camden Street from 1852–1974. James Pearse, father of Patrick and Willie, worked there, and Jack's father knew Willie well from the College of Art. Beautiful examples of Earley stained glass are to be found in the Star of the Sea church in Sandymount, Mount Argus monastery in Harold's Cross, and the church of St Thérèse, Mount Merrion.

Jack was still a schoolboy in January 1941, and his memories are very definitely those of a young person. His first and emphatic statement about the bombing was that there had been no serious injuries. He identified where exactly the bombs had fallen and pointed out that, had they fallen on the road, the cobbles (or setts) on which the tram lines were laid would have acted as shrapnel, and the damage and loss of life could have been most grave.

The explosion drove in the door of the Earley house and, with the subsequent after-draft, sucked glass and curtains onto the road and from the chimneys drew soot that covered the floors. The front room ceiling was damaged, as was the return of the house, which had to be rebuilt. While the house was still technically habitable, the children were sent to stay with relatives in the area. Jack moved to Parnell Road, just to the south of the terrace, over the canal, but decided after a few days to move back home. The official contractors had arrived within a few days, but Jack remembers them being there 'nearly until Easter', 13 April in 1941. For some time soldiers blocked access to South Circular Road from the Barracks entrance to Sally's Bridge, but they soon got to know the residents, including Jack and his parents, and there was no problem in getting to and from the house. He doesn't remember even missing school for the period.

What Jack remembers well is the paraphernalia of war in Dublin. There were several bomb shelters in the area: in Lennox Street just up from Leonard's Corner, an underground one in Oscar Square, another to the north in the area called Fairbrother's (or the Tenters') Fields, and one in the barracks across the road. There was also a large one in Dame Street, where the Central Bank is now. The Dublin shelters were big – 'as big as two or three rooms' – and could take quite a number of people. Jack never remembers them being used during raids. Instead they became playgrounds for the boys of the area in the immediate aftermath of the war, until they became too unsavoury even for them to use, when they were abandoned and the Corporation demolished them. He also remembers the ARP delivering seven gas masks to the household – one for every resident. Another recollection is that the soldiers who helped clear the synagogue found quantities of tea and sugar there, just as Mick Synott reported above. Jack continued his education in the College of Art in the 1950s, and while his memories of Donore Terrace in the war years are certainly interesting, his stories of the Dublin art world of the period are quite fascinating.

Finlay and Chris Myles – Oscar Square and Rialto[14]

Finlay and Chris Myles both grew up along the South Circular Road; Finlay was a schoolboy at the time of the bombing, Chris is younger. She lived in Oscar Square, about 800 metres from the blast. Her memories – and this pattern is even further evidenced by those of her husband – show how local the destruction was. She was kept awake all that night by the noise of the bombers overhead, and the massive explosion just before 4 a.m. terrified her. The next day, with her sisters and companions she made her way along St Thomas Road and the badly damaged Dufferin Avenue to review the destruction. The soldiers and Gardaí on duty kept them from actually entering the South Circular Road, but they could go to the corner and see the enormous crater. Finlay, growing up a mere two kilometres away in Rialto, was aware of nothing. Again, both dismissed as ridiculous the story that the synagogue had been targeted, but once more the story of the tea and butter stored there was recounted by both, and both remembered their elders telling how they felt that the shine of canal water had confused the pilots.

Chris remembered two large air raid shelters within a few hundred metres of her home – the underground one in the square itself and another in Weaver Square, a short distance to the north-west. Again, they have no memory of them ever being used. While Finlay's aunt's house in Wolseley Street suffered somewhat badly – the ceilings collapsed – the only damage to Chris' home, a few hundred metres further away, was that the windows to the rear were broken. Her father simply replaced them himself.

To summarize, then: Paddy Culligan went back to work (albeit briefly) that very afternoon, and, while Finlay Myles in Rialto heard nothing, Chris Myles heard the bombing and saw its results, but her own house was hardly touched. Jack Earley alone experienced some of the destruction caused by the two bombs. Taken together, the stories perhaps show why the event features so lightly in accounts of the period – it really was a very local bombing.

5. Belfast, Easter 1941

While the south was officially neutral in the war, Northern Ireland, as part of the United Kingdom, was deeply involved, particularly through ship-building. In spite of this, precautions against air attacks were pitifully inadequate, and there was almost a total lack of preparedness, with few air raid shelters and a woeful lack of anti-aircraft guns.[1] Indeed, the Unionist government had refused an offer of extra fire fighting equipment made by London in 1941. To compare with those in power in Dublin, it must be stated that the opportunities of the Northern government to be informed of the awful power of the Luftwaffe were fewer, given that they would have known almost no volunteers – Catholic or Republican – from the Spain of two years earlier.

The extent of their incompetence was made dreadfully clear on the night of 15/16 April 1941, when several hundred German bombers, flying from newly conquered bases in northern France, dropped nearly a quarter of a million bombs, high explosive and incendiary on Belfast. The damage was extensive and the response of the fire service and ARP pitifully inadequate in spite of the enormous efforts of the personnel involved. On the very eve of the bombing, the *Irish Times* reported that the Belfast Union Commissioners were told that only 14 applications for fire watchers had been received by the Clerk. They required 'about 70'.[2] It was clear that reinforcements were needed, but the closest British service of any size was in Scotland – clearly out of the question. That left a possibility that was unpalatable in the extreme, involving a city that many Unionists regarded as hostile, and, what was worse, asking for help from a southern politician who was known and disliked in equal proportions: de Valera. The Ulstermen came up with a solution: they phoned Hernon.

What happened next is detailed in a double-page of foolscap covered in hand-written notes in pencil, quite in contrast with his normal precise record keeping, and put by the city manager in a small file consisting mostly of correspondence dealing with strikes in the Corporation.[3] At 5.10 a.m. he received a phone call from Belfast, in which a request was made for urgent fire brigade assistance from Dublin in fighting fires in Belfast. Hernon first phoned his fire chiefs, Comerford and O'Sullivan. Then (the note says 'at the same time') he phoned the Taoiseach and informed him. De Valera said it was 'a serious matter', and would seek advice. At 5.50 a.m. the Taoiseach phoned back telling Hernon to give any assistance possible. The city manager phoned

Major Comerford to this effect. Then de Valera rang again, telling Hernon that
he should make sure it was of sufficient importance, and instructing him to
confirm who had made the call. The city manager called the Belfast supervisor
of public telephones, who told him that the call had come from the
commissioner of police who had made it on behalf of the 'Ministry of Public
Security'. This meant that the call was made on the authority of John
McDermott, described by Seán McMahon as being 'more aware of the realities
of the situation than his complacent, elderly, colleagues'.[4] McMahon tells how
McDermott consulted with the Northern Ireland Deputy Prime Minister, Sir
Basil Brooke. Aware of the sensitivities of dealing with a regime they found
unacceptable and a politician they disliked, McDermott took the decision to
phone 'the Town Clerk' of Dublin. This would indicate that Hernon was
contacted by virtue of his position rather than his reputation. At 7.30 a.m.
Hernon recorded that he had informed the Taoiseach that three pumps (two
fire brigades and one AFS) had left and two more were getting ready – one
each from Dún Laoghaire and Dundalk. Another from Drogheda is recorded
in pencil.

Perhaps conscious of the possible implications of helping belligerents, the
southern papers were remarkably coy in recording the events. The raid was
covered extensively, but the involvement of the firemen from Dublin and the
other towns got hardly a mention. Likewise conscious of the sensitivities, their
role was not extensively covered on the neighbouring island either.
Nonetheless, and again giving lie to the canard that 'everything was censored',
the *Northern Whig* on the next day, 17 April, reported that 'it was confirmed
in Dublin this morning that units of fire-fighting and ambulance services from
some towns in Eire assisted to put out fires resulting from Northern Ireland's
blitz'. And that same day, the *Irish Times* in an uncensored editorial expressed
with approval the fact that:

> Humanity knows no borders, no politics, no differences of religious
> belief. Yesterday for once the people of Ireland were united under the
> shadow of a national blow. Has it taken bursting bombs to remind the
> people of this little country that they have common tradition, a common
> genius and a common home? Yesterday the hand of good-fellowship was
> reached across the Border. Men from the South worked with men from
> the North in the universal cause of the relief of suffering.

On 19 April de Valera's speech in Castlebar received widespread coverage:

> This is the first time I have spoken in public since the disaster in Belfast
> and I know you will wish me to express on your behalf and on behalf
> of the Government our sympathy with the people who are suffering

there ... they are all our people, they are one and the same people, and their sorrows in the present instance are also our sorrows. I want to say that any help we can give them in the present time we will give to them wholeheartedly believing that were the circumstances reversed they would also give us their help wholeheartedly.

An initial reading of this might lead one to question the Taoiseach's prudence, as it was tantamount to telling the Germans that Dublin would always help Belfast. Yet over 20 years later, Eduard Hempel, envoy extraordinary and minister plenipotentiary of the German Government in Dublin, told an interviewer that 'nobody from Germany protested, and I had no intention of doing so'.[5]

Two sets of events might be regarded as being clarified by the history of that dreadful week. De Valera's well-known good relations with Hempel might show why the Irish government could be so overt in their aid. And that overtness, tinged with not even the slightest hint of condescension nor the slightest triumphalism, might explain the behaviour of Belfast when, two weeks later, that city was again bombed. This time the northern response was both more pragmatic and more immediate. Hernon was again involved, and again recorded the events, this time neatly typed in a one-page *aide de memoire* dated 5 May 1941.[6]

But on this occasion the call did not come to him. Belfast contacted de Valera directly in response to this attack, and it was the Taoiseach who phoned the city manager. And that call for help was almost immediate, for Hernon's first intimation was just after midnight.

12.30 a.m. Taoiseach 'phoned me and stated that Belfast had again been attacked. Told me to be prepared to send assistance if called upon to do so.

12.40 a.m. 'Phoned Major Comerford and told him to be on the alert.

12.45 a.m. Taoiseach rang again and stated that the Brigade should travel in daylight, if possible, but if an urgent message was received, we would have to take the risk and go. No men to be sent who had not volunteered. I told him that some members of the AFS would have to go. In the case of an accident to any of these men legislation would have to be introduced to deal with the matter.

2.25 a.m. Taoiseach rang and stated that all available fire assistance which could be spared was to be sent to Belfast. Stated that the police and military were to be informed so that the way would be clear for the Brigade. Also stated that we should confine our activities to rescue from private houses rather than military objectives.

2.35 a.m.   Rang Major Comerford to this effect. He stated he would send
              an ambulance with 4 men and Superintendent Gorman and
              an engine with 8 men making a total of 13 men, in 15 minutes
              after receipt of my call.

2.45 a.m.   Call from Belfast. Line very bad. Informed Supervisor,
              Telephones, Dublin to convey message re military and police.
              This had to be done via Portadown.

3.15 a.m.   Rang Major Comerford and told him to instruct his officers
              regarding rescue from private houses rather than military
              objectives, as stated by the Taoiseach. Major Comerford stated
              that it would be impossible to do this, but the utmost care
              would be taken to do it diplomatically if possible, and he was
              instructing his officers to this effect.

              Rang Mr O'Mahoney, Dun Laoghaire, and asked him to be
              ready to assist.

3.30 a.m.   Rang Mr O'Mahoney and told him to get ready to send an
              ambulance and to see that his men volunteered for this duty.

3.40 a.m.   Rang Major Comerford again. He stated that 13 men had gone
              on two vehicles and 11 were ready to go on two more, that
              one crew each from Dún Laoghaire, Drogheda and Dundalk
              were proceeding to Belfast, together with two AFS crews and
              two pumps from Headquarters, Tara Street.

Hours of Departure

Dual appliance and ambulance	3.21 a.m.
4 Units	4.40 a.m.
Dún Laoghaire	4.40 a.m.
Lorry and medium unit	9.55 a.m.
Staff car (Major Comerford)	9.55 a.m.

25 Regular and 29 AFS volunteers (Approx. twice the assistance
sent on the previous occasion)

Appliances Sent

    9 pumps, consisting of
    6 pumps and ambulance from Dublin with 53 men (29 A.F.S.
    and 24 R.F.B.)
    1 pump from Dun Laoghaire
    1 pump from Drogheda
    1 pump from Dundalk

7 a.m.   Message received from Superintendent Gorman from Belfast – 'Fires out of hand. Send 17 men and pump.'

The following ambulances were also sent:

6 a.m.   2 Ambulances from St John Ambulance Brigade containing 10 men

8 a.m.   3 Ambulances from Red Cross

While at no stage is there even the slightest hint of criticism of any aspect of the Northern Irish response, Hernon could not been unaware of the shambles that met his men in Belfast, and would have noted the acknowledgment made by McDermott of this help, an appreciation delivered in Stormont on 22 April:

> I should also like to take this opportunity of expressing my appreciation of the help so readily given from outside this country. As part of the United Kingdom we knew we should expect its full sympathy and support in any suffering which the Battle of Britain would impose upon us. The help afforded by our southern neighbour, Eire, was not related to any bond of war or to any political consideration. It was above and beyond politics. It was based on a common humanity, and we gratefully accepted and acknowledge it as such.[7]

The Minister's nationalist opponent, Thomas Campbell (like McDermott, representing a Belfast constituency) echoed the praise:

> There have been manifestations of goodwill and practical generosity and sympathy from across the Border, and we should not conclude to-day without an expression of our earnest and grateful acknowledgment of those manifestations. One touch of nature makes the whole world kin.

6. The aftermath

Six weeks later the skills so quickly developed by Dublin's fire and ARP personnel, and the organizational abilities of Hernon and his staff, had their greatest test. On the night of 31 May 1941, four high-explosive bombs were dropped on the North Strand area of Dublin City.[1] This time the casualties were much more severe, with 28 killed and 90 injured. As with the January attacks, a folklore grew up about this incident as well – either it was a deliberate ploy by Hitler's government to force neutral Ireland into the war or as a reprisal for the assistance given by Dublin Fire Brigade during that Belfast Blitz of a few short weeks previously.

The Irish Red Cross provided emergency shelter for people made homeless by the bombing at the Mansion House and in parish halls throughout the city. Meanwhile, Dublin Corporation was responsible for clearing the North Strand area and providing permanent alternative housing for the victims. Charleville Mall Public Library was designated as the headquarters for the bombed area and, again, O'Rourke was given charge of the clearance project. Many of the residents here, however, were far less well-off than their fellow citizens across the city. The Corporation decided that it would provide accommodation for all people from bombed areas; the word 'temporary' was pencilled-in before 'accommodation'. Without choice, those needing accommodation were re-located to the new Dublin Corporation housing estates at Cabra and Crumlin.[2]

Two crucial differences in approach were taken by the Corporation: the number of authorized contractors was vastly increased, and any claim for compensation had to be submitted and approved before work could begin. This standard form made the task of restoration much more manageable.[3]

The demographic profile of the area, as well as the appalling damage and loss of life, were almost certainly factors in those affected being far slower in responding. O'Rourke was able to wait until 4 June – four days after the bombing – to inform the contractors of this position.[4] The fact that there was a local, single point of contact for the residents – Charleville Mall Library – also meant that issues could be dealt with speedily and without undue correspondence. The success of this new approach is perhaps best shown by the fact that, out of over 3,700 houses affected, there were only 130 (two of which were in the area most affected) that were repaired by the owners/occupiers.[5] In the Donore bombing, the figures were 668 (of which two were demolished, and five owned by the Corporation) repaired by official contractors versus 104 done privately.[6]

By far the most dramatic change between the January incidents and the later bombing began with a letter from Moylan to the city manager dated 13 June 1941, where he said 'I visited the North Strand on 12 instant and to say that I was amazed and shocked at the lack of progress is to put it lightly'.[7] He continued: 'the demands of public morale that the matter be dealt with swiftly could only be met by putting sufficient labour, equipment and directional staff on the work'. The deputy city manager wrote to O'Rourke on 14 June, passing on Moylan's comments and asking for a report by the following Monday.[8] On 16 June O'Rourke responded to that letter.[9] He had acted with the greatest possible promptitude; every available official had been pressed into service as well as ten contractors, two quantity surveyors and five private architects. Then, perhaps in a comment a more prudent employee might not have made, the city architect reminded his superior that he had written to him the previous year pointing out that preparations should have been made then for such an eventuality, but nothing had been done. It is, perhaps, unwise to remind one's superior of correspondence they might prefer not to recall, for on the following day Hernon wrote two letters, filed together in the folder.[10] One letter appointed R.S. Lawrie, chief warden in the Air Raid Precaution Department of the Corporation as officer in full control of repairs of bomb damage in the North Strand. The city architect, Lawrie was told, had been informed and the chief ARP warden could take over immediately and completely. The other letter, to the city architect, expressed Hernon's complete dissatisfaction with O'Rourke's lack of progress and his 'obvious reluctance' to carry out instructions. The city architect was, consequently, removed from the work in question, and his successor was Lawrie.

That the move came as a surprise to O'Rourke is shown by a perfectly business-like memorandum written by him the same day to Hernon describing the progress on the work in North Strand.[11] Hernon, in a handwritten comment, states that it was 'received after interview with me and after having handed over control to Mr Lawrie'. As he had done earlier in Donore, O'Rourke then put on file a précis of operations both justifying his response and defending his actions.[12] Pointedly, it is clear from the stamp on the document that the copy on file ended up in Lawrie's department.

From this point also one sees, either explicitly in the original or as an annotation, that correspondence with O'Rourke on the Donore bombing – still officially his responsibility – was forwarded more and more to Lawrie: for example letters on 18 July 1941, 21 August 1941, 26 January 1942 all have the ARP warden's name on them.[13] Additionally, when correspondence such as that already referred to, such as Keane's letter of 25 February 1942, was being forwarded to outsiders, it becomes clear that O'Rourke was being sidelined. It was obvious that O'Rourke was out, and Lawrie was in. Furthermore, Lawrie was now clearly in the driving seat in both areas. In a handwritten note dated 8/9/41 the city manager discussed the matter of *all* quantity surveyor fees with Lawrie who agreed to take the matter up with the surveyors, and Lawrie was able to report to Hernon on 14 October that the Minister concurred with terms close to those he had agreed.[14] Hernon's reliance on and appreciation of his ARP warden is perhaps clarified by a handwritten note included with the Belfast material referred to above. In a slightly chaotic pencil-written set of notes to himself, one cartouche stands out. It simply says: 'Mr Lawrie 75954. 5–30 Saving Life. Humanitarian Grounds'. The number is Lawrie's phone. There is no indication as to who said what. What is obvious is that the city manager consulted one whose views he trusted and whose opinions he valued.[15] In defence of Lawrie, it must be said that almost all the improved efficiencies in the latter bombing were of his doing. The application form just mentioned, for instance, was an initiative of his a mere four days after his appointment, and it is clear that he managed the North Strand campaign with great ability.[16] By 23 December 1941, Mr J. Sherwin of the housing section of the Corporation was able to write to D.J. Redmond in the Department of Finance. On all three bombings – Terenure, Rialto and the North Circular Road – the expenditure to date had been £120,200 and he estimated an additional £40,000 for repairs, £5,000 for furniture etc., and £50,000 for acquiring North Strand properties for a total of £215,200, or, in Sherwin's words, 'say £220,000'. This is quite remarkably close to O'Rourke's estimate, nearly a year previously, of £250,000 for the January bombing and all subsequent ones. The file contains no detailed breakdown of the figure for Rialto.

On 18 May 1942 O'Rourke could finally write to J.P. Keane of the finance section that only one claim remained which had received no payment whatsoever, and this was a disputed matter.[17] On 3 June the Department replied there were no grounds for making an exception in this case. With this note the files end. The residents who had left began moving back to their repaired homes relatively quickly. But not all returned: of the 34 houses with residents, only 25 had the same surname on the Voters' Register in 1945.[18]

Three years later, O'Rourke retired as city architect at the end of June 1945.[19] The situation in his office for those years must have been of some delicacy, for, unlike Colonel Thomas E. Gay (his colleague in ARP), Lawrie was not an army officer – he was an architect in Dublin Corporation, and O'Rourke was his superior. The position of city architect was not filled immediately, but, at the end of 1946, Lawrie returned to his native Scotland and the following year Conor McGinley was appointed as O'Rourke's successor.[20] Was Lawrie, perhaps, the chosen candidate, but decided not to take the position?

In 1942 Hernon was given the additional responsibility of being manager of Dublin County, and 13 years later, after serving as city manager for over 18 years, insisted on being allowed retire in 1955, against the wishes of the Corporation.[21] It will be remembered that while they had opposed his original appointment, they now wished him to continue in office. His was the longest period of service as city manager and town clerk in Dublin Corporation/City Council.

His letter of resignation was read at the meeting of the City Council on 2 May of that year.[22] The Lord Mayor, the redoubtable Alfie Byrne, seconded by Councillor Michael J. O'Higgins TD, proposed that the city manager be asked to reconsider, and this was 'put and carried'. Hernon's gracious refusal was read at the meeting a month later, on 6 June, and his resignation was accepted with regret.[23] Then followed a series of laudatory statements by aldermen and councillors praising his service. The praise was echoed by the staff through the person of the assistant city manager, T.C. O'Mahony. The motion, with the wishes of the council for continued good health and many happy years of quiet, restful and well-earned retirement, was put and carried unanimously.

There were no similar expressions of appreciation recorded 11 years previously when O'Rourke stepped down. He had had the misfortune of dealing with residents of steely determination and equally versatile contractors and surveyors, and was, in the end, worsted in the game. However, had he waited in that bitterly cold January to get a proper plan with proper controls in place, the recriminations would have been equally reproachful, and far more justified. Through his skills and ability, the first significant disaster in war-time Ireland was dealt with speedily and efficiently, albeit not as thriftily as it might have been, and lessons were learned for the North Strand six months later.

THE REASONS

There is still some discussion as to exactly why Dublin was bombed.[24] Opinion at the time included the almost equally ludicrous suggestions that the Germans deliberately bombed Ireland in order to get it into the war on the British side, thereby providing Germany with an excuse to invade, and that the bombs had really been dropped by British pilots flying captured German aircraft and they were, in addition, using captured German bombs. One modern author has suggested that the opposite theory to that first conjecture might be correct: that the aim was to convince 'Eire', as he calls it (without the accent), to remain neutral. He then comments that if this be true, their actions were clearly successful. Any meaningful analysis of this most interesting proposition, however, is made more difficult by the fact that no discussion of the matter could be found on the pages cited in either of the two works mentioned in the accompanying footnote.[25]

During the Luftwaffe campaign of 1940 and 1941, Germany used a number of radio direction systems to guide their bombers to their targets. The popular belief has been that British attempts to jam these radio signals resulted in German aircraft dropping their bombs off-target (i.e. on Dublin) or that the British were able to disrupt the beams such that they led the bombers onto a specific target; in his history of the Second World War, Winston Churchill stated that the bombing of Dublin 'may well have been an unforeseen and unintended result' of the campaign. The suggestion has been discussed by several writers, most comprehensively by Richard Hawkins.[26] Hawkins demonstrates that this was so unlikely as not to justify serious consideration. It has been shown that at that time it was only possible to disrupt and confuse the German bomber crews over a very short range, and certainly never actively control them.

Further it must be recognized that, at this stage of the war, and despite their radio assistance aids, it could still be difficult for a German bomber crew to find their way to their assigned target. The *Irish Independent*, in December 1945, after the war reported on a press conference the previous week in the British Ministry of Information.[27] RAF chiefs of telecommunications disclosed details of intercepted German radio messages, including one where a bomber reported being over Peterborough when the crew were actually over Central London. The officers continued that the real reason Dublin was bombed was not because German planes were sent there by 'purposeful mistake', but through the bad navigation of inexperienced pilots. One of the incidents mentioned in the opening chapter of this work may serve to corroborate this view. The devices dropped on the morning of 1 January near Kilmacanogue in Wicklow were magnetic mines. But such mines are designed for dropping at sea – they are naval mines placed in water to destroy ships or submarines.[28] That these were dropped several kilometres inland shows that the pilot's awareness of his location was, to say the least, problematic.

Finally, the explanation of two of those interviewed for this book, and who remembered the period, is given again; both Paddy Cuilligan and the Myles suggested that the sheen of canal water had confused the bombers. While an initial response might well be dismissive, this rationale might equally be applied to the North Strand, where the area bombed was beside the Royal Canal. No one, it appears, has linked the proximity of the canals to both bombings, and discussed this possibility.

Meanwhile, back on the South Circular Road, life went on. On 4 June 1941, some days after the North Strand bombing, a letter was sent to the Department of Foreign Affairs, and forwarded to Finance.[29] The owner of a house in Haroldville Avenue, off the South Circular Road, reported that her property had been damaged in the 'heavy bombing attack on Saturday', and could compensation be organized. She was referred to the Corporation. In the *Irish Times* of 13 November 1941, Lee's, no. 99 on the terrace, was offered to let 'seen by appointment'.[30] Whatever damage it had suffered the previous January, by the end of that year it was in a condition to be put on the market. And a week before, in the *Weekly Irish Times* of 8 November a notice appeared:

> Sharpe and Morelli – August 26 1941, at St Theresa's, Donore Avenue, with Nuptial Mass and Papal Blessing, John, of 127 South Circular Road to Adelina, only daughter of Mr and Mrs A. Morelli, 119 Donore Terrace.[31]

Life went on.

Conclusion

The conclusion of these events was finally marked in Dáil Éireann on 8 June 1971, almost 30 years to the day since the North Strand bombing:

Dáil Éireann – Volume 254 – 8 June 1971
Ceisteanna – Questions. Oral Answers. – North Strand Bombing Compensation.

Mr Harte   asked the Minister for Finance if he will state in respect of a claim for compensation made against the German Government in 1941 in connection with the bombing of the North Strand, Dublin, whether any compensation was received; if so, the date it was received; and how it was disposed of.

Mr Colley: Compensation totalling £327,000 approximately was received from the Federal Republic of Germany in respect of the bombing in 1941 of the North Strand, Dublin. The final payment was made in 1958. The compensation was paid into the Exchequer.

Mr Harte: Have any of the families who lost members received any compensation?

Mr Colley: Yes. They were compensated, in fact, from the Exchequer. That is why the money was paid into the Exchequer, because it was recovered later. Details of this were laid before the Dáil in 1959.

Mr Harte: Did the Minister say the money was paid out in 1959?

Mr Colley: I said the details of the agreement between the two Governments were laid before the Dáil in July, 1959, but the people concerned had already been compensated by the Government here.

Mr P. Belton: Was the amount paid by the Exchequer greater than the amount paid by the West German Government?

Mr Colley: Yes, greater. It was £344,000 as against £327,000 recovered.

And so it ended. The dramatic events of the North Strand have been the subject of books, theses and articles. The corresponding story of the bombing of Donore Terrace, touching as it did the lives of a relative few, would be far less remarkable had the area affected been merely those 35 houses. The story of the large number of Dubliners whose property suffered damage becomes interesting when one considers the immediacy and the similarity of their response; within hours of the incident they saw that, properly dealt with, someone, the Corporation or the state, would compensate them for their loss. The pursuit of that compensation, both by individuals and groups, was single-minded and focused. The immediate response of the Corporation – to get the affected houses habitable again – was to be complimented given the time of year in which the bombing happened. But the rather paternalistic approach of the officials, particularly Howard O'Rourke, was totally unsuitable to dealing with an articulate, educated, middle-class group of affected citizens. The tensions between O'Rourke and his superior, the city manager, were also unhelpful. Nonetheless it is clear that both men, and many of their Corporation colleagues, saw themselves as being part of a coherent organization 'serving the city', and believed and trusted in the motto of that organization: *obedientia civium urbis felicitas* (obedient citizens make a happy city). Were that true, Dublin would have been, and perhaps would still today be, a most sad town.

Appendix 1

DONORE TERRACE AS RECORDED IN *THOM'S* 1941, THE EVACUATION LIST AND THE 1940/41 VOTERS' LIST:

Number	Thom's	Evacuation List	Voters' Register
85	Price, Thomas	3 Prices	3 Prices
87	Foran, Mrs M.	Mrs Foran and 2 other ladies	no voter
89	Leventhal, S.	3 Leventhals and Cecil Lee who shared a business address with Harry Leventhal, Dr & Mrs Elliman and Miss M. Griffin	3 Leventhals and Cecil Lee who shared a business address with Harry Leventhal
91	Day, George	2 Days and 2 Stephens and Miss Reddy	2 Days and Marjorie Stephens
93	Roith, Rev. M.	7 Roiths and Miss Keane	3 Roiths
95	Cavey, J.	3 Caseys [recte Cavey] and Miss Regan	4 Caveys and Eva Doyle
97	Turner, H.S.	Mrs Gilbert, 4 Turners and Mr & Mrs Colum	2 Turners and Henrietta Gilbert
99	Finnegan, J.J.	9 Finnegans	6 Finnegans
101	Fox, Simon	7 Foxes Mr Marks and Miss Wilson	2 Foxes and a female, Ella Benson
103	Kenny, Robert D.	2 Kennys	2 Kennys and May Daly
105	Price, C.	6 Prices and Miss McKeown	6 Prices and Mary Foley
107	Brown, Miss	3 Browns and Mrs Donner	3 Browns and Elizabeth Murray
109	Cooper, W.	Vacant	2 Coopers and Eileen McNiece
111	Chamberlain, Mrs A.	Not vacated	2 Chamberlains

Number	Thom's	Evacuation List	Voters' Register
113	Smyth, Dr James	Not vacated	2 Smyths
115	Sevitt, A.	Not vacated	6 Sevitts and a female, Nancy Evers
117	Kennedy, Patrick	Not vacated	3 Kennedys
119	Morelli, Louis	Not vacated	6 Morellis and Annie Ahern
119a		Not vacated	2 Burgesses
119b		Not vacated	2 Hewitts and 2 Grahams
86	Marcus, I.	4 Marcuses and Miss Purcell	5 Marcuses
88	Woolfson, Mrs	3 Ellisons	3 Ellisons and 2 Woolfsons
90	Clein, Lewis	2 Miss Cleins, 3 ladies and 2 gentlemen	2 Cleins and Bridget Lynch
92	Lipschitz, Leo	The Lynn family and Molly Miller	2 Lipschitzes and Molly Miller
94	Mann, Joseph	4 Manns and 4 Rosenbergs	4 Manns
96	Lazarus, H	5 Lazaruses, Mr & Mrs Greene and Miss Nugent	2 Lazaruses and a female, May Mahoney
98		2 Dalys	2 Dalys
100	Synagogue		no voter
102	Hayman, M.	2 Haymans 2 Gurries and 4 others	3 Haymans and 2 others
104	Earls, Mrs	2 Earls	2 Earls
106	O'Donnell, Patrick	2 O'Donnells	2 O'Donnells
108	Summers, Dawson	2 females – Summers and Nugent	3 females – Summers, Nugent and Dunwoddy
110	Bolger, Mrs H.	Mis McCullagh and Miss Bolger	3 McCullaghs and Miss Bolger
112	Lynch, Wm.	Not vacated	3 Lynches and Elizabeth Lawless
114	Young, Mrs Mary	Not vacated	2 Youngs and 2 Doyles
116	Kerr, Robt. Wm.	Not vacated	3 Kerrs
118	Reardon, J.P.	Not vacated	4 Reardons

Notes

ABBREVIATIONS

ARP Air Raid Precautions (Service)
DCA Dublin City Archives
LDF Local Defence Force
LSF Local Security Force
MA Military Archives, Cathal Brugha Barracks, Rathmines, Dublin
NA National Archives Dublin

INTRODUCTION

1 Edward Freeman, *The methods of historical study: eight lectures read in the University of Oxford* (London, 1886), p. 148.
2 Georg G. Iggers, *Historiography in the twentieth century: from scientific objectivity to the postmodern challenge* (Middletown, CT, 1997), p. 108.
3 Sigurdur Gylfi Magnusson, 'What is microhistory?' on the History News Network web site, http://hnn.us/articles/23720.html, accessed 19 September 2009.
4 Ibid.
5 Bernadette Cunningham, & Raymond Gillespie, *Stories from Gaelic Ireland: microhistories from the sixteenth-century Irish annals* (Dublin, 2003); Carlo Ginsberg, *Il formaggio e i vermin* (Turin, 1976); Robert Laffont, *La grand massacre des chats* (Paris, 1985); Angela Bourke, *The burning of Bridget Cleary* (New York, 1999).
6 *Irish Independent*, 4 Jan. 1941.
7 DCA, *The North Strand bombing*, CMD/1941/2.
8 Ken Howarth, *Oral history* (Gloucester, 1998), p. viii.
9 Howarth, *Oral history*, p. 3.
10 Jennifer Cannon Duffy, 'The Corporation of Dublin and the bombing of the North Strand, 31 May 1941' (NUIM, MA thesis, 2002).
11 Irene Wilson Power, *To school in the city* (1997), p. 33; Catherine Scuffil (ed.), *By the sign of the dolphin: the story of Dolphin's Barn* (Dublin, 1993).
12 Tony Gray, *The lost years: the Emergency in Ireland, 1939–45* (London, 1997).
13 As quoted in Gray, *The lost years*, p. 147.
14 Report in *Neue Zürcher Zeitung*, Aug. 1942; quoted in Helen Litton, *The World War II years: the Irish Emergency, an illustrated history* (Dublin, 2001), p. 111.
15 James Meenan, 'The Irish economy during the war' in Kevin B. Nowlan and T. Desmond Williams (eds), *Ireland in the war years and after: 1939–1951* (Dublin, 1969), pp 28–38.

1. DONORE TERRACE, A BRIEF HISTORY

1 Donore Terrace is now the name of a small *cul-de-sac* off South Brown Street, about 900 metres north of the original.
2 Subsequently Richmond, then Wellington, then Griffith Barracks; now Griffith College.
3 *Thom's Dublin Street Directories*, (Dublin, 1880–).
4 *Thom's* (1880–97).
5 NA, Census of Ireland 1911; available online at http://www.census.national

archives.ie/search/, accessed 30 May 2009.

6 NA, Census of Ireland 1911, http://www.census.nationalarchives.ie/reels/naio00156213/, accessed 21 Sept 2009. Figure for no. 98 seems questionable.

7 NA, Census of Ireland 1911, http://www.census.nationalarchives.ie/reels/naio00156203/, accessed 21 Sept. 2009.

8 *Thom's* (1941); DCA, Dublin City Council, Voters' registration registers for Dublin City *1939–45*. online resource.

9 DCA, CMD/1941/1 folder 2 Donore area bombing.

10 DCA, CMD/1941/1 folder 2.

11 DCA, CMD/1941/1 folder 4. A folder of many 'bundles'; top item in this bundle dated 28 July '41.

2. THE BOMBING

1 Under the 1937 Constitution, the name of the state was Éire (or, in the English language, Ireland). The UK government accepted that it was no longer the Free State, but, unwilling to use the name Ireland for the 26 Counties, used 'Eire', without the accent. e.g. the Eire (Confirmation of Agreements) Act 1938 (182 Geo.VI, c.25).

2 *Irish Times*, 21 Oct. 1997.

3 Historical debates web site, http://historical-debates.oireachtas.ie/D/0077/D.0077.193909020007.html, accessed 15 Aug. 2009.

4 Eunan O'Halpin, *Defending Ireland: the Irish state and its enemies since 1922* (Oxford, 1999), p. 156.

5 Air Raid Precautions Act, 1939. No. 21/1939.

6 The Stationery Office, Dublin (1939).

7 Pádraic O'Farrell, *Down Ratra Road* (Dublin, 2000), p. 3.

8 Civil Defence Ireland, http://www.civildefence.ie/cdweb.nsf/documents/AEEB06284977F81C80256E8A003C631F, accessed 1 July 2009.

9 O'Halpin, *Defending Ireland*, p. 156.

10 Henry Patterson, *Ireland since 1939* (New York, 2002), p. 39; Jonathan Bardon, 'The Belfast blitz, 1941' in Dermot Keogh & Mervyn O'Driscoll (eds), *Ireland in World War Two* (Cork, 2004), pp 259–73.

11 MA, G2/X/0468, Second World War bombings, Campile bombing.

12 MA, G2/X/0468 folder 4; letter dated 16 Sept. 1940 but signed on 17 Sept.

13 Air Raid Precautions Act, 1939, section 60.

14 Ruth McManus, *Dublin 1910–1940: shaping the city and its suburbs* (Dublin, 2002), p. 49; Archiseek – online Architectural Resource, http://www.archcirc.com/buildings_ireland/dublin/city_development/oconnell_street.html, accessed 30 June 2009; Archiseek, http://irish-architecture.com/buildings_ireland/dublin/city_development/abercrombie_1941/index.html, accessed 30 June 2009.

15 History of Dublin City Council, http://www.dublincity.ie/YourCouncil/AbouttheCouncil/Pages/DublinCityCouncilHistory.aspx, accessed 30 June 2009.

16 Dublin City Public Libraries and Archives, *Serving the city* (Dublin, 2006), p. 47.

17 DCA, CMD/1941/1 folder 1.

18 *Irish Press*, 21 Dec. 1940.

19 All detailed in MA, G2/X/619, Second World War bombings, Jan. 1941 bombings.

20 High explosive.

21 MA, G2/X/619 headed 'Bombing at Donore Terrace, S.C.Rd., Dublin on 3 Jan., 1941'.

22 *Irish Independent*, 3 Jan. 1941.

23 *Irish Independent*, 4 Jan. 1941.

24 MA G2/X/619, signed L.A. 3/1/40.

25 DCA, CMD/1941/1 folder 2. The dated and signed copy is the 2nd one filed.

26 *Irish Independent*, 4 Jan. 1941.

27 NA, S12062, Department of the Taoiseach, European War 1939: bombing of Irish territory by foreign aircraft.

28 *Irish Press*, 3 Jan. 1941.
29 William Brazier, The work of an air
    raid warden, Dublin 1942 (handwritten
    notebook and maps); DCA, Class
    number: 941.83, New Street.
    RCN:EX00039677.
30 *Irish Times*, 4 Jan. 1941.
31 *Irish Times*, 6 Jan. 1941.
32 *Sunday Independent*, 5 Jan. 1941.
33 Historical debates web site,
    http://historical-debates.oireachtas.ie/
    S/0024/S.0024.194005290009.html and
    http://historical-
    debates.oireachtas.ie/S/0024/S.0024.19
    4009250004.html, both accessed 26
    June 2009.
34 DCA, CMD/1941/1 folder 2. Referred
    to in memorandum dated 9 Jan. headed
    Re: ARP bomb damage repair and in a
    memorandum dated 16 Jan. from
    O'Rourke to Hernon, receipt ref. 449.
35 DCA, CMD/1941/1 folder 2, headed:
    Memorandum of meeting between the
    city manager.
36 DCA, CMD/1941/1 folder 2, dated 4
    Jan. but filed with material from 10 Jan.
37 DCA, CMD/1941/1 folder 2 dated 6
    Jan. 1941, headed ARP structural first-aid.
38 DCA, CMD/1941/1 folder 2 dated 9
    Jan. 1941 headed Re: ARP bomb
    damage repair.
39 DCA, CMD/1941/1 folder 2 dated 7
    Jan. 1941, ref. TAH/H.
40 DCA, CMD/1941/1 folder 2.
41 DCA, CMD 1941/1 folder 2.
42 DCA, CMD/1941/1 folder 2,
    'memorandum to city manager & town
    clerk re: bomb damage repairs'.
43 Ibid.
44 All in DCA, CMD/1941/1 folder 1.
45 Copy in DCA, CMD/1941/1 folder 2,
    receipt 873.
46 DCA, CMD/1941/1 folder 2.
47 DCA, CMD/1941/1 folder 2. Nos. 85,
    87, 89, 95, 97, 99, 101, 103, 105, 107, 109
    on the south side of Donore Terrace,
    and 84, 86, 88, 90, 92, 94, 96, 102, 104,
    108 and 110 on the opposite side, and,
    across the canal, 41 Parnell Road.
48 DCA, CMD/1941/1 folder 2. Receipt
    acknowledged 21 Feb. 1941; ref. 1524.

49 See first chapter: List of A. Grimston,
    DCA, CMD/1941/1, folder 2.
50 DCA, CMD/1941/1 folder 2.

3. REPAIRING, REDECORATING,
RECRIMINATIONS

1   DCA, CMD/1941/1 folder 2.
2   DCA, CMD 1941/1 folder 2, headed
    'Structural first-aid' and marked
    O'R/MP.
3   DCA, CMD/1941/1 folder 2 headed
    'Re: ARP'.
4   DCA, CMD/1941/1 folder 2,
    memorandum to city manager and
    town clerk.
5   DCA, CMD/1941/1 folder 2, filed
    with 29. Ref. H 1234/5/1941, receipt
    818.
6   DCA, CMD/1941/1 folder 2.
7   DCA, CMD/1941/1 folder 2.
8   DCA, CMD/1941/1 folder 2, ref.:
    F.18/4/41. Typescript dated Márta 1941,
    although filed between material dated
    27–8 Feb., headed Damage by bombs
    etc.
9   NA, S0263, Department of the
    Taoiseach, Seanad 1937; nomination by
    Taoiseach 1938 (1 Seanad, under Act 16
    of the Constitution).
10 DCA, CMD/1941/1 folder 3, last item
    in bundle beginning 28 July 1941.
11 Seán T. used both versions of his
    surname: O'Kelly and Ó Ceallaigh.
12 NA, S12160, Taoiseach's Office,
    Emergency war measures: damage to
    property, temporary repairs and
    compensation.
13 NA, S12160, but filed later than (above
    in the bundle) the previous item cited.
14 NA, S12160.
15 DCA, CMD/1941/1 folder 4, small
    bundle beginning 7 Aug. 1941.
16 DCA, CMD/1941/1 folder 2.
17 DCA, CMD/1941/1 folder 2 ref. H.
    1234/24/41.
18 DCA, CMD/1941/1 folder 2.
19 DCA, CMD/1941/1 folder 2, marked
    in red 'Copy for information of city
    manager'.

20 DCA, CMD/1941/1 folder 2, filed in an out-of-sequence group under 8 May.

21 All in DCA, CMD/1941/1, folder 3.

22 DCA, CMD/1941/1 folder 4; bundle beginning 5 May 1941, letter dated 1 May 1941.

23 DCA, CMD/1941/1 folder 2.

24 DCA, CMD/1941/1 folder 2, receipt 4430.

25 DCA, CMD/1941/1 folder 2, ref. H.1234/44/41.

26 DCA, CMD/1941/1 folder 4, small bundle beginning 17 June 1941, letter dated 13 June 1941.

27 DCA, CMD/1941/1 folder 2, dated 7 Jan. 1941.

28 e.g. DCA, CMD/1941/1 folder 2, dated 14 Jan. 1941.

29 NA, S12160, notice which appeared in the public papers on 13/1/41l; *Irish Independent*, 13 Jan. 1941.

30 DCA, CMD/1941/1 folder 4, bundle beginning 14 July 1941.

31 DCA, CMD/1941/1 folder 3.

32 DCA, CMD/1941/1 folder 4, bundle beginning 14 July 1941, letter dated 21 Jan. 1941, ref. 84.

33 DCA, CMD/1941/1 folder 4, same bundle, letter dated 14 Feb. 1941, ref. 84.

34 DCA, CMD/1941/1 folder 4, same bundle, letter (from Montgomerys) dated 9 Feb. 1941.

35 DCA, CMD/1941/1 folder 4, letter dated 29 July 1941.

36 DCA, CMD/1941/1 folder 4, bundle beginning 14 July 1941.

37 e.g. DCA, CMD/1941/1 folder 2, 9 Jan. 1941.

38 Historical debates web site, http://historical-debates.oireachtas.ie/D/0081/D.0081.194102050005.html, accessed 15 Sept. 2009.

39 All in DCA, CMD/1941/1, folder 4.

40 Historical debates web site http://historical-debates.oireachtas.ie/D/0084/D.0084.194107080016.html, accessed 15 Sept. 2009.

41 DCA, CMD/1941/1 folder 2, note re: bomb damage repairs, dated in pencil, initialled PJH.

42 DCA, CMD/1941/1 folder 2.

43 DCA, CMD/1941/1 folder 2.

44 DCA, CMD/1941/1 folder 2, receipt 6126.

45 DCA, CMD/1941/1 folder 2, ref. H.1234/43/41.

46 DCA, CMD/1941/1 folder 2, received 17 Sept. 1941, receipt 7737.

47 DCA, CMD/1941/1 folder 5, ref. H.15563/6/41.

48 DCA, CMD/1941/1 folder 5, ref. H.15663/19/41, dated 7 Aug. 1941.

49 DCA, CMD/1941/1 folder 5, ref. H.1234/50/41.

50 DCA, CMD/1941/1 folder 5.

51 DCA, CMD/1941/1 folder 5, receipt 10661.

52 DCA, CMD/1941/1 folder 4, small bundle.

53 DCA, CMD/1941/1 folder 4, bundled with above.

54 DCA, CMD/1941/1 folder 2, 25 Feb. 1942.

55 DCA, CMD/1941/1 folder 2, 20 Mar. 1942, ref. H.693/2/41.

56 DCA, CMD/1941/1 folder 2, ref. H.11460/1942.

4. THE FOLKLORE

1 DCA, folder 35–37166. http://www.dublincity.ie/Recreationan dCulture/libraries/Heritage%20and%2 0History/Dublin%20City%20Archives/ Collections%20Post%201840/Pages/do nore_bombing_archives.aspx, accessed 1 July 2009; O'Halpin, *Defending Ireland*, p. 157.

2 BBC, 'WW2 People's War', http://www.bbc.co.uk/ww2peopleswar/storie s/54/a6084254.shtml, accessed 1 July 2009.

3 Benjamin Grob-Fitzgibbon, *The Irish experience during the Second World War: an oral history* (Dublin, 2004), p. 127.

4 Grob-Fitzgibbon, *The Irish experience*, p. 220.

5 Billy French, *Memories of my Ireland gone forever* (Dublin, 1997), pp 185–95.

6 Seosamh Ó Broin, *Inchicore, Kilmainham and District* (Dublin, 1999), pp 248–9.
7 Wilson Power, *To school in the city*, p. 33.
8 Scuffil, *By the sign of the dolphin*, pp 112–13.
9 BBC, 'WW2 People's War', http://www.bbc.co.uk/ww2peopleswar/, accessed 6 June 2010.
10 Interviewed by author 23 June 2009. Transcribed the same evening.
11 DCA, CMD/1941/1 folder 2, letter dated 3 Jan. 1941, Lawrie to Hernon.
12 *Irish Press*, 4 Jan. 1941.
13 Interviewed by author 30 May 2009. Transcribed that evening.
14 Interviewed by author 6 July 2009. Transcribed that evening.

5. BELFAST, EASTER 1941

1 Seán McMahon, *Bombs over Dublin* (Dublin, 2009), p. 75.
2 *Irish Times,* 16 Apr. 1941.
3 DCA, CMD, file no. 1.
4 McMahon, *Bombs over Dublin*, p. 75.
5 *Sunday Press*, 8 Dec. 1963, as quoted in T. Ryle Dwyer, *Behind the green curtain* (Dublin, 2009), p. 159.
6 DCA, CMD file no.1, item 7, p. 1.
7 'The Stormont Papers: 50 Years of Northern Ireland Parliamentary Debates Online': http://stormontpapers. ahds.ac.uk/stormontpapers/pageview. html?volumeno=24&pageno=641, accessed 6 Feb. 2010.

6. THE AFTERMATH

1 DCA, CMD/1941/2 the North Strand bombing.
2 DCA, CMD/1941/2 folder 1.
3 Cannon Duffy, Corporation of Dublin, p. 31.
4 Cannon Duffy, Corporation of Dublin, p. 29.
5 Cannon Duffy, Corporation of Dublin, p. 23.

6 DCA, CMD/1941/1 folder 3, report of 21 June 1941.
7 DCA, CMD/1941/2 folder 1.
8 DCA, CMD/1941/2 folder 1.
9 DCA, CMD/1941/2 folder 1.
10 DCA, CMD/1941/2 folder 1.
11 DCA, CMD/1941/2 folder 1.
12 DCA, CMD/1941/2 folder 1, dated 17 June.
13 All in DCA, CMD/1941/1 folder 2.
14 Both in DCA, CMD/1941/1 folder 5.
15 DCA, CMD file no. 1, item 6, p. 2.
16 DCA, CMD/1941/2 folder 1.
17 DCA, CMD/1941/1 folder 2.
18 DCA, 1945 voters' register.
19 'Irish architectural archive', http://www.dia.ie/architects/view/421 3, accessed 11 June 2009.
20 'Irish architectural archive', http://www.dia.ie/architects/view/552 8, accessed 19 Sept. 2009; DCA, 'List of city architects', desk copy.
21 DCA, *Serving the city*, pp 47–8.
22 DCA, Minutes of the Municipal Council of the City of Dublin 1955, item 110.
23 DCA, Minutes of the Municipal Council of the City of Dublin 1955, item 156.
24 See in particular Clair Wills, *That neutral island* (London, 2007), pp 210–12.
25 Brian Girvin, *The Emergency: neutral Ireland, 1939–45* (London, 2006), p. 180, ftnote 80.
26 Richard Hawkins, '"Bending the beam": myth and reality in the bombing of Coventry, Belfast and Dublin', *Irish Sword*, 19 (Dublin, 1993–4), pp 131–43.
27 *Irish Independent*, 5 Dec. 1945, 'London letter'.
28 Dr Ian Speller – pers. comm.
29 NA, F018/0092/41, 'Bombing at North Strand Dublin on 30 May 1941', Dept. of Finance (filed Dept. of External Affairs).
30 *Irish Times*, 13 Nov. 1941.
31 *Weekly Irish Times*, 8 Nov. 1941.